# Walking the Spiritual Walk

## A Successful Search for Purpose and Partner

by Carolyn Kresse Murray

A.R.E. Press • Virginia Beach • Virginia

Copyright © 1994
by Carolyn Kresse Murray
1st Printing, July 1994
Printed in the U.S.A.

All rights reserved. No part of this book may be reproduced or transmitted in any form or by any means, electronic or mechanical, including photocopying, recording or by any information storage and retrieval system, without permission in writing from the Publisher.

A.R.E. Press
Sixty-Eighth & Atlantic Avenue
P.O. Box 656
Virginia Beach, VA 23451-0656

Quotations from *A Search for God* are taken from the 50th anniversary edition, A.R.E. Press, 1992.

Biblical quotations are taken from the King James Version.

Grateful acknowledgment is made to the following publishers for permission to reprint from their publications:

*Complete Poems, 1904-1962*, by e.e. cummings. Liveright Publishing Corporation. New York, N.Y.

*God Calling*, by A.J. Russell. Published by Barbour & Company, Inc., P.O. Box 719, Uhrichsville, OH 44683.

*The Kingdom Within*, Revised Edition, copyright 1987 by John A. Sanford. HarperCollins Publishers. New York, N.Y.

*A Life of Jesus the Christ: From Cosmic Origins to the Second Coming*, copyright 1989 by Richard Henry Drummond. HarperCollins. New York, N.Y.

"Walking," copyright 1948 by Theodore Roethke. From *The Collected Poems of Theodore Roethke* by Theodore Roethke. Used by permission of Doubleday, a division of Bantam Doubleday Dell Publishing Group, Inc.

*Why Jesus Taught Reincarnation*, copyright 1992 by Herbert Bruce Puryear. New Paradigm Press. Scottsdale, Ariz.

Library of Congress Cataloging-in-Publication Data
Murray, Carolyn Kresse, 1962-
    Walking the spiritual walk : a successful search for purpose and partner / by Carolyn Kresse Murray.
    p. cm.
    ISBN 0-87604-324-4
    1. Murray, Carolyn Kresse, 1962- . 2. Association for Research and Enlightenment—Biography. 3. Nurses—United States—Biography. 4. Spiritual life. I. Title.
BP605.A77M87 1994
299'.93—dc20
[B]     94-18154

Edgar Cayce Readings © 1971, 1993 by the Edgar Cayce Foundation.
All rights reserved.
Cover design by Ravenwood Studios

TO TOM

The Man Who Shares the Spiritual Walk with Me

## TABLE OF CONTENTS

Preface ................................................................... ix
Acknowledgments ............................................. xiii
1  No Chance Meetings ................................... 1
2  The Road Home .......................................... 18
3  The Beach .................................................... 30
4  Beyond Convention .................................... 38
5  Star Crossed ................................................ 48
6  First a Dream .............................................. 56
7  Searching for God ...................................... 71
8  For Love of a Friend .................................. 86
9  Village of Faith ........................................... 102
10 Heaven on a Sister's Arm ......................... 114
11 Without Bounds ......................................... 121
12 Moving Mountains .................................... 129
13 Dew upon the Flower ............................... 136
14 Beginnings ................................................. 148
15 From the Mouths of Babes ...................... 157
16 Awaiting the Gift ....................................... 168
17 Slaying Dragons ........................................ 176
18 Till We Meet Again ................................... 185

# *Preface*

THE search for meaning and purpose is universal. Religion, natural science, philosophy, medicine, and psychology all manage to fill and feed different aspects of that need. We ask big questions, and sometimes the answers we discover satisfy us for the moment. Still, we continue to ask and seek and occasionally find.

I am a work in progress. When I clarified what the central purpose for my life is, I was surprised to discover that it is not defined by career choices, volunteer activities, or how I spend my leisure time—although all of these are encompassed by it. However I express my purpose in my day-today life changes, my commitment is stronger at times than others. Yet I can look to it for light when I'm uncertain of choices and decisions that must be made. I look to my mission for clarity. That mission is simply to grow closer to the God I am trying to serve and in the process learn the art of loving.

The biggest question that I face now is a daily "Does this—action, inaction, word, silence, etc.—bring me closer to or further away from the Holy Spirit?" The specifics of my theology become less and less important as I gauge my success by whether or not I am closer to Him.

To understand where I've been and where I think I'm going, it is necessary to speak first of the influences that have molded my way of looking at the world. The first is Jesus Christ. In Him I eventually found my reason for living.

The Christian church planted seeds that were almost choked out by weeds of doubt as I grew confused about traditional theology. I loved Him, but I couldn't shake the feeling that part of the story was missing from my Sunday school lessons. That's where a second influence came to resurrect my faith.

Edgar Cayce, a prophet of recent times, touched me through his legacy of psychic readings. Those readings are the written accounts of his answers to questions posed to him during a self-induced trance state. It was not mediumship. He was not channeling disembodied spirits, but rather tuning in to a universal source of information.

Cayce became aware of the healing power of his psychic readings after suffering from complete laryngitis as a young man. Having exhausted the medical options available to him, he decided to try hypnosis. The hypnotist was successful in putting him under and instructed Cayce's body to heal itself. Edgar Cayce later found that he could place himself in this altered state of consciousness at will and tap into knowledge that was mind boggling and encompassed a broad range of subjects. A questioner could ask anything and the sleeping Cayce would answer.

The readings initially dealt with medical problems. After he successfully recommended interventions to restore his own voice, the gift blossomed to include suggestions for family, friends, and others suffering from various disorders. His abilities were remarkable. Having only the name of the individuals and where they would be during the reading, he could describe their surroundings explicitly, as well as the specifics of their problem and measures to relieve it.

The readings focused on spiritual realities as well, and he always maintained that acknowledging the mind, body, and spirit connection is imperative in achieving health. Eventually, the advice took an even more unconventional turn when the subject of reincarnation came through during a session. A devout Christian, Cayce had read the Bible once through for every year of his life, and it disturbed him that his gift had introduced a concept that at first seemed heretical. He had always felt a bit freakish in his odd role, but carried on the work which he believed was part of the mission he had been promised in a childhood vision. This new development added even more reason to feel trepidation among his Christian friends.

With maturity came the realization that reincarnation was not such an outlandish idea after all, and he continued to teach Bible study and conduct readings for the many suffering people who contacted him. Edgar Cayce died in 1945. Fortunately, those readings were recorded and preserved for future generations to study and apply in their own lives.

My knowledge of Cayce and his readings began in grade school. After reading some of the classic books that detailed his life and work, I felt I'd found the missing pieces that had been lacking from my personal philosophy. Later, as an adult, I joined a Search for God study group, a program Cayce had begun while he was alive.

The purpose of the study group program is to bring together small groups of people interested in studying spiritual principles and putting them into practice in their lives. Meditation, prayer, and daily disciplines helped me grow and develop my own abilities as a disciple of Christ. The fellowship of the group also made me feel less alone in my search and provided an underpinning of strength that enabled me to face everyday conflict.

*Walking the Spiritual Walk* is the account of some of the experiences that have shaped my faith. Since the walk is less lonely when shared by another with the same goal in mind, it is also a story of finding a partner to laugh and cry with. Someone to link strengths and join hearts with in an attempt to do the work He calls us to do. A friend, a lover, a mate for my soul.

This is my Love story. Family, husband, friends, and acquaintances have portions of their stories intermingled with mine. It is their laughter and love that have brought me closest to knowing my God. I now humbly share them with you.

# ACKNOWLEDGMENTS

Writing a book is never a purely solitary process. I wish to thank all those who shared the experience with me. To Joe Dunn, publisher of A.R.E. Press, for giving me the opportunity to tell my story; and my editor, Ken Skidmore, for adding the humorous touch that helped to make revisions a pleasant task.

Special appreciation goes to all of the family and friends who allowed me to unabashedly include anecdotes involving them. In particular, Greg, Tim, Jeff, and Jason, four little boys who are quickly entering the potentially embarrassing age of adolescence—I'm grateful for the permission they gave me as their aunt to speak freely.

Many thanks go to my mom and dad for giving me room to explore and take the risks that create far more interesting real-life plot twists; and for always being there with open arms. I also thank my Murray mom and dad for their extraordinary love and acceptance.

I would like to express gratitude to a spiritual and literary mentor, the late Catherine Marshall. Her words have lifted me many times, helping me to see the adventure and marvelous potential of the Christian life. If this book inspires someone even one-tenth the way her work inspired me, it has achieved its purpose.

Finally, to Tom, who supported me the most during the last year as I struggled to get down on paper the essence of what he and so many others have taught me of the value of intimate relationship. For his being willing to have our relationship made transparent in an attempt to reach the hearts and spirits of others like us, I am grateful to him.

# 1

## No Chance Meetings

> "My beloved spake, and said unto me, Rise up, my love, my fair one, and come away."
> —Song of Solomon 2:10

THE idea of a personal destiny waiting to be discovered has always fascinated me. This destiny is not apart from but enmeshed with our choices and decisions. It is not an arbitrary predetermined force that operates without benefit of our own creativity, nor a blank canvas awaiting only our own sweeps of color to bring it to life. Rather, destiny is a cooperative energy set in motion by desire and acts of our will that builds over time until one day the fruit appears, much to our delight, perfectly ripened. Destiny is an immense power forged from the partnership between a soul and its Maker.

On a clear October day in 1985, I boarded a 747 to begin to meet mine. Long before the wings of that jet could lift, however, the stage was being set for the answer to my prayers for a life partner. It was being set for my date with destiny.

A year or so before that colorful autumn weekend excursion, I sat entranced during an evening lecture at Unity church in Springfield, Illinois. Following a childhood spent discovering orthodox Christianity alongside the voluminous psychic readings of Edgar Cayce, I was ever eager to learn more about the spiritual path we're on with its twists and turns and never-ending opening doors. While my walk was not always traditional in theological views, it continued to take place alongside Jesus Christ, my choice of guides.

That night I learned a technique for creating positive changes in my life. The instructions were simple: Amidst quiet, baroque music (a style that enhances relaxation), repeat positive affirmations in a clear, soft voice into a tape recorder. The teacher explained that the desirability of using a self-made rather than professionally recorded tape is that the subconscious mind, accustomed to hearing each person's own voice rather than a stranger's, is more likely to incorporate those suggestions into waking consciousness.

The hypothesis behind this quasi-hypnotic regimen I was learning about was not new to me. I had long held an interest in the study of the mind-body connection and strongly believed that what we feed into our minds eventually manifests itself in the physical world. Yet I had rejected the idea that it is desirable to focus on what we want and pour our energy into its materialization. That type of practice produces a wish-list spirituality, and my desire is to be open to God's unlimited ideas for my life. I took what I needed from the teachings that evening and chose to see these affirmations as prayers that would open me to what

God already had planned and waiting.

It was with a mind free of skepticism that I sat one afternoon next to my stereo as it played Vivaldi's *Four Seasons,* while I softly whispered the affirmations into my tape recorder. The two prayers most important to me were: "Attract to me the people whom I need in my life now" and "Draw to me that special soul whom I will love, help, comfort, and bring joy to, the one who will also love, help, comfort, and bring joy to me."

What was the motivation behind this grand experiment? I desired a man who would share my passion for living. I had made some poor choices while testing my wings, choices I allowed to happen due to unconscious, sometimes contradictory motivations. I now wanted to consciously let my love life be guided by my own ideals of love and service and, without making specific demands about the person I wanted in my life, allow God to direct my path to the man most suited for me. A new graduate nurse, I returned each morning after working the night shift at St. John's Hospital to place my tape recorder next to my bed and drift off to sleep amidst soothing, inspiring words and music.

For many months I continued my tape-playing practice. I was lonely for someone to laugh with, talk to, and share my dreams with. I was lonely for a man, yet hesitant about rushing into a relationship. I had for the most part distanced myself from the night life scene in order to dedicate more time for study and meditation with as unclouded a vision as possible. I was alive with enthusiasm for the Truths that I was discovering in my personal seeking and with my small spiritual study group. Yet I felt torn because there really weren't any near my age group in the gatherings I moved among and few of the opposite gender. It frightened those I met in traditional churches when I mentioned some of my unconventional interests in the paranormal, although I tried not to let the fact that I subscribed to beliefs somewhat out of the ordinary become a big issue in my own mind or anyone else's whom I might meet.

The Cayce readings had introduced many new ideas into my personal philosophy, and it was hard for me to leave out the concepts that had brought so much sense and such a feeling of "Yes!" to my questioning heart. This Edgar Cayce was a simple man of God who discovered that there is a realm of spirit just outside our normal waking senses that is waiting to be tapped into by all of us. I learned that the old stereotypical crystal-gazing fortune tellers were not a true representation of how a genuine psychic operates. Most important, the wisdom I found in the readings led me away from a fearful theology full of hellfire and brimstone into one of love and service, and I was cautious not to sacrifice this in the dash for a relationship.

Sometime earlier I had experienced this type of romantic disappointment. One afternoon while browsing in a little Christian bookstore known as "The Mustard Seed," I met a young man my age who had been recently "converted" from a wild life style spent partying heavily into the strict confines of a fundamentalist church. I could identify with his sense of disillusionment with a way of living that placed which clubs to frequent on Saturday night at the top of the priority list. Yet I knew that on a right-to-left religious continuum, we were far apart.

The strong attraction between us overruled my hesitation, and since I wanted a shared faith so badly, I plunged ahead. I decided to work hard at emphasizing our agreements and sidestep any conversation that included concepts which might disturb his new-found faith.

We dated for a few weeks. I often accompanied him to a coffeehouse near my apartment that served up heaping spoonfuls of "Repent and Be Saved" theology with their espresso. I remained silent and inwardly cringed. I could feel my blood pressure rising as I suppressed the urge to take to the pulpit myself! I longed to share the love of an all-forgiving Father who does not will that any of His children be lost, but has prepared a way out—and not only through an uttered prayer of allegiance to one particular church. I began to realize that denying my own experience of who God is in favor of someone else's was hypocritical. I had to be myself and risk losing my new boyfriend.

One evening after a dinner of spaghetti and meatballs, we sat in my kitchen rapt in discussion. Gingerly, I began to present a case for alternative spiritual studies. I started out mentioning biblical prophets whose ideas had rocked the religious leaders of their times right out of complacency and into a fight for their own power. Jesus was one of those and by far the most outspoken. The closer I got to present-day people of God who walked a less well-trodden road than the rest of us, the further away my friend grew from me. I could see in his eyes that all the warnings he'd been filled with about Satan and his messengers had built too strong a wall for me to tear down, and for my part I could never return to that place of fear in my own life. Our paths, with all their potential similarity, were at the moment too drastically different to reconcile. I continued alone, saddened by the loss of a friend I had truly enjoyed spending time with, yet with a sense of liberation for having spoken from my heart.

That New Year's Eve was spent in the home of a fellow spiritual seeker, far away from toasts and midnight kisses. Four women of completely different backgrounds and age groups gathered together to release the old and bring in the new. We had a candlelight communion service, much prayer, and inspired messages for all from one of the women. I felt refreshed and renewed by the event, but at the same time I needed my peers, and a little romance. Yet my loneliness was not overwhelming or all-consuming. It was somehow sweet, because my love affair with Jesus

Christ was unfolding more and more. Spurred on by the readings' loving guidance, I was attempting to follow the Master wherever He wanted to lead, and an "I can wait" attitude lived within my heart; I just wasn't sure for how long.

Whether due to my pre-sleep tapes or my own romantic heart reaching full term, 1985 began an exciting year for me. I visited Hawaii in the spring (ignoring an intuitive draw towards Israel to spare family members excessive worry), and quit smoking shortly thereafter with the help of pre-sleep suggestion tapes. Summer included friends and barbecues by the pool at the new apartment I shared with another nurse named Penny, a fellow spiritual explorer.

Then fall arrived, bringing mildly cool breezes to highlight the golden days and take the edge off the blazing summer's end. One warm September evening I went with a few co-workers to a bar frequented by the hospital crowd, "Biggies and Bubbas." I was becoming bored and just about ready to leave when I noticed a familiar face, one of the medical interns named Taras from our hospital. He and I struck up a conversation, consisting at first of the usual hospital-oriented small talk. As we stood in the crowded bar, our interest ventured into the areas of psychic phenomena and the Edgar Cayce readings, and at once I was wide awake. He was actually familiar with this work that had consumed me for so long.

These remarkable compilations of dialogues recorded while Cayce assumed a trance state were food for exciting thought and talk. Questions asked of this "sleeping prophet," as he has become known, brought amazing answers that have kept people studying and researching their contents since their beginning over ninety years ago. With his integrity scrutinized numerous times by reputable investigators, he has never been successfully discredited. Most of the early readings concerned medical problems, but as time went on they grew to encompass spiritual matters as well. Cayce died in 1945, but the organization that he founded, the Association for Research and Enlightenment, Inc., lives on vibrantly.

My studies of the readings were intense, but somewhat isolated; so finding a peer with a similar interest was wonderful. As it later turned out, he was only minimally versed in the material, but that common denominator had launched a friendship nonetheless. Little did I know that it would be a channel for changing the course of my life or perhaps just a helper to steer it where it was already headed and preparing to go anyway.

We spent evenings in deep discussion munching Mexican food, and it led to some very interesting discoveries, particularly his ideas about "animal attraction" in humans. He explained that his belief is that people who look alike tend to gravitate to one another (he based his theory on scientific observations involving animals!). Laughter, coupled with a growing trust and sense of connection between the two of us, helped prepare me for the turn of events soon to surprise me.

It was a few weeks later, sitting in the cafeteria at the hospital, that I playfully ribbed Taras further. "So, who do I look like, or should I ask what do I look like?" I joked. He and I certainly didn't resemble each other, and we had already determined that ours was to be a friendship, not a love match. "It's funny you should ask that," he began in a serious tone. "I've had a feeling for a while now that you should meet my friend in New York, Tom Murray." Very intrigued, I said that I would think about it.

I did not connect this rapidly evolving arrangement with my affirmations, however, because it had been quite awhile since I had used the tape and I wasn't focusing on results. I was in that autumn sort of mood when excitement is in the brisk air, with leftover feelings of joy and anticipation due to years of returning to school and friends (I still can't resist buying myself some pencils and folders each year) deeply embedded in my consciousness. It sounded irresistible to experience such an unusual blind date in the exotic setting of New York. Still, it was a scary prospect to be three days in the family home of someone I had never met.

A few days later we were out driving when Taras pulled into the Kitty Hawk Travel Agency and arranged for my flight to New York City. I had a three-day weekend approaching, and the plane fares were extremely low at that time. Things were moving quickly, and there really wasn't much time for internal debate. The ticket was mine, and, as he said, if Tom and I didn't hit it off romantically, at least we would each have another person in this world to call friend.

I listened to Taras testify on behalf of Tom Murray's respectability and moral character, and heard a report of his own visit to Tom's home. My faith in Taras's apparent intuition in other areas of his life also influenced my decision to trust his judgment. Finally, being a twenty-three year old with an adventurist nature, I couldn't say no. Inside, the lights were flashing bright green as the final details were ironed out for me.

Meanwhile, Taras had further scheming to attend to with the other human half of his match. A Chicago native with Ukrainian roots, he easily took to arranging potential love connections, and his powers of persuasion are legendary among his friends. My slightly olive-toned skin and a streetfull of relatives in a largely Italian neighborhood were enough evidence for him to assume a heritage for me that he believed would be a fitting lure for Tom. Assuming that my blood flowed from Rome, he added Catholicism to my bio as the perfect finishing touch. I was unaware of the intricate, but somewhat inaccurate picture he was painting.

The fun of planning the trip overpowered my usual tendency toward introspection. I was caught up in the nervous decision-making spiral of what to wear, what to say, and what to expect from this most unusual blind date. Yet with all the excitement there were still moments spent in the quiet of prayer. This centering helped me to step out in what may have seemed to some a risky proposition.

I worked the 3:00 to 11:00 p.m. shift the evening before the Big Day. When I arrived back at the apartment, Penny and our good friend Leslie were up waiting for me. They were driving me the ninety miles to St. Louis the next morning (my plane left at dawn). We girl-talked for a couple of hours, and it was quite late by the time I crawled beneath the covers. Sleep was elusive as I lay there tantalized by wakeful dreams of Tom Murray. Despite my sleeplessness, on October 4, 1985, I was on my way to meet my mystery man.

Time moved in light-year fashion, and soon I could hear the pilot announcing our descent. Yes, it had been a rush of events, but the beads of sweat on my forehead signaled that it was really just the beginning. I had carried along my favorite devotional book, the one volume I would choose to have with me if I could have no other. Its title: *God Calling*. It contains comforting, inspiring words spoken by Jesus to two women of this century who sought His presence. The writers remain anonymous, the editor—A.J. Russell. It's as if Jesus is speaking the words directly to the reader; I gain a tremendous sense of His caring from this little paperback. This time, however, I was frantically flipping from page to page, attempting in vain to quiet my mind and nerves as the plane began its slow-motion landing, and my pulse skyrocketed from 72 to 120! The plane did touch ground, and I somehow managed to avoid cardiac arrest, leaving me with mere palpitations and cold sweats.

Feelings of loneliness were far behind as I gathered my belongings and made my way out into an unknown milieu of possibility. I almost wished for a return of their familiar easiness and predictability while experiencing the height of my apprehension. Solitary confinement began to seem a welcome alternative to this increasing build-up of anticipation.

Suddenly, there he was! He was carrying a sign so that I would recognize him, the type that business people hold high with their company names emblazoned on them when meeting an unfamiliar client. But I knew him. He kissed my cheek and led me away to pick up my bags, then on to the parking lot and his big, shiny green 1978 Ford Thunderbird. I immediately felt at ease with this man and began telling him of my soaring pulse rate during landing. He liked to laugh, and within seconds my nervousness transformed into an ear-to-ear smile.

We rode and chatted like friends reunited at long last. I was struck immediately by his sense of humor and quick wit. His gorgeous hazel eyes and thick dark hair didn't hurt matters any either. I soon noticed that he was never at a loss for words, something that I admire in others because I can become quite self-conscious and tongue-tied in tense situations such as this one. It was too soon to tell, but we seemed to fit. Our mutual matchmaking friend was right—we bore a resemblance to one another. I was definitely feeling good with this cute Scottish-Italian New Yorker.

I felt as if I were on another planet upon entering New York City. It was so overwhelming—the buildings with their intricate architecture, the sounds of horns honking and people yelling, the gridlocks of the streets in which Tom had remarkable maneuvering ability. I felt like a tiny country mouse as we weaved our way through the maze with the towering frames surrounding us. It was wonderful. After spending the rest of the day sightseeing and sipping drinks in the World Trade Center, we found ourselves in a cozy but crowded restaurant enjoying a buffet and really talking for the first time.

"So, which authors are your favorites?" was the question

he asked upon discovering our common love of story. Then on to the title of my most loved book. I explained that it was lodged in the backseat of his car and that later he could have a look for himself. Since I didn't want to seem too "religious" at that point, I decided not to venture into an explanation of its contents. After all, this was our first meal together.

We joked some more as we slowly became acquainted, and I learned of his allergy to shrimp. It was nice discovering someone else for the first time, uncovering his likes and dislikes and each other's odd little idiosyncrasies. He explained that he loves shrimp and regrets the fact that his body doesn't react well to the shellfish (he could see that I love it, too, and it was almost as if he were apologizing for not being able to enjoy it with me). With a generous style that I was soon to learn is his trademark, he brought back a plateful for me to gorge upon. He was quite the gentleman that evening, extending a chivalrous hand of a friendship.

After dinner it was on to the movies to see *Agnes of God*, starring Jane Fonda, a film I had chosen. He held my hand in the long line outside the theater and stood very close to me. The next thing I knew his arm was around me, and I was getting pleasantly nervous. I'm very shy, but he didn't share in my self-consciousness, and so I felt relieved once inside the theater with the comforting blanket of darkness to help me feel more at ease. I had that nice, slightly tense sort of feeling that usually accompanies a first date, as we cuddled romantically in our seats. I later learned that he comes from a very demonstrative family, and I love it. Afterward, he wanted to talk about the movie, and I was impressed by his intelligence and insight; it was an adventure just talking to him. We wandered the streets hand in hand, and once more I felt that I was in another world.

We got back to his parents' home on Long Island quite late, and I met his mom and dad (how many get to do that on a first date?!). I was in awe. His mother looked like a movie star, black hair and slim body—absolutely beautiful. She reminded me of the actress Rita Moreno. Mr. Murray had such a sweet Scottish charm about him that it was easy to see where Tom had learned to treat a lady so well. They were hilarious enough in bantering back and forth that I began to feel as if I were part of a television sit-com. It was like a fairy tale for me being allowed into their home for the weekend. I felt very blessed.

The next morning Mrs. Murray made bacon and eggs and endured heckling from her two sons about her cooking skills (the food was actually quite delicious). Bob Murray seemed a lot like his older brother, and both revealed a sharp wit in dealing with Momma Murray, which was well reciprocated. After a picture-taking session we loaded into the car for a full day of seeing the sights in the Big Apple. As Tom shuffled papers in the backseat of his car, his eyes landed on my little companion, *God Calling*. He asked if it was the book I had mentioned as my favorite the night before, and incredibly it turned out that he also owned a copy that he read every night and even brought with him on some of his travels.

I was excited, but soon astonished at the message awaiting us. As I began to read the passage for that day, October 5, I saw the title "No Chance Meetings." I read further:

> The Lord shall preserve thy going out and thy coming in from this time forth, and even for evermore. (Psalm 121:8)

> All your movements, your goings and comings, controlled by Me. Every visit, all blessed by Me. Every walk arranged by Me. A blessing on all you do, on every interview. Every meeting not a chance meeting, but planned by Me. All blessed. Not only now, in the hour of your difficulty, but from this time forth and for ever-

more. Led by the Spirit, a proof of sonship. "As many as are led by the Spirit of God, they are the Sons of God," and if children then heirs—heirs of God. What a heritage! Heirs—no prospect of being disinherited. "Heirs of God and joint heirs with Christ: if so be that you suffer with Him that you may be also glorified together." So your suffering has its purpose. It is proof of Sonship. It leads to perfection of character (the being glorified), and to Union with Me, God, too. Think of, and dwell upon, the rapture of this. (Russell, 1978)

Despite having read the book on the plane, despite having known about the trip in advance, I hadn't read the passages for that weekend. I instead had done what I usually do, opened the book at random, to no day in particular. We both felt a slight shock wave, but neither of us gave voice to that feeling. The look that passed between us was all that was necessary. It was a day kissed by October sunshine as we drove to the train station, multicolored leaves scuffling in the breeze. It was good.

The Museum of Natural History was our first stop. With wire-rimmed glasses, crisp shirt, and skinny leather tie, Tom looked very much the part of sexy scientist as he shared glimpses of ancient civilizations with me. Dinosaur bones dwarfed us, poised for eternity in midstep. More aware of my companion than my surroundings, I could have been anywhere and felt goose bumps. Consequently, I hold more fond remembrances of *Tyrannosaurus rex* than one might normally expect!

A mosaic of painted tiles depicting colorful scenes surrounded Grant's Tomb, the next tourist spot on our list. An image of a castle in the center added a magical touch. We marveled at the painstaking work of the artist who created this oasis of beauty to delight visitors. Giant oaks just beginning to display leaves tipped in gold graced the background.

At the top of a cathedral, we stood next to a huge and very old bell. As Tom snapped pictures, the wind blew through an open window and lifted my long hair from my shoulders while it fanned out behind me. Again, he kissed my cheek with a tenderness that warmed me. The entire day was glorious, sunny enough for only a sweater or light jacket and filled with new sights of a city I had until then seen only through the lens of someone else's camera.

The majesty of St. John the Divine Cathedral was breathtaking. Massive archways and pillars once again dwarfed us as the dinosaur bones had. New York was like a mountain range, making me realize how magnificent the entirety of creation, even made by humans, really can be. I felt at home with my arranged date as we toured the second church of the day. I was becoming more accustomed to his touch and frequent kisses as we played throughout the afternoon.

By dusk we had finally made it to Columbia College, Tom's alma mater, in the center of Harlem. It was thrilling to visit such a well-known and respected institution, but the real joy was in imagining Tom walking to classes or studying near a tree. The images in my mind were very much "college brochure" in their focus—not quite grounded in reality. Nearby I had my first taste of falafel, the garbanzo bean-filled pita bread concoction so well known to New Yorkers. I savored it as I munched and studied my date a little more.

Walking the streets later that night, we were approached by a homeless man asking for money to help his sick daughter. Whether his story was true or not didn't matter, we both dug into our pockets to help him and were rewarded with a kiss on the cheek for me and a promise of lighted candles and prayers for both of us. We walked and explored late into the night, ending up in Greenwich Village sipping beer and listening to a group singing show tunes around a piano.

Those are a few of the images that remain so poignantly

with me. I simply have to "pull up" onto the screen in my mind thoughts of that weekend and instantly I can feel a bit of the excitement that I felt then. Sometimes I think I can even sense the sun on my face exactly as I felt it that day. Later, when we faced rough times both together and apart, it helped to recall the magical nature of our meeting.

I was, nevertheless, beginning to have some negative impressions. Low self-esteem reared its ugly head as I entertained the notion that somehow I wasn't worthy of Tom. It wasn't due to anything he said or did; it was just an old familiar fear that originated within me. He was becoming almost saintly in my eyes, and I was becoming sad. I felt that I couldn't measure up to him, didn't "deserve" him. It seemed to me he had always studied hard and helped other people. He had such an intensely kind way about him; he exuded integrity. It wasn't until later that the picture I had of him included more realistic images of a down-to-earth, real person, complete with flaws. For the moment I was being swept away in an illusion of sorts, nice for falling in love, but not altogether without danger.

That night we went to the Orpheum Theater for the off-Broadway musical production of *Little Shop of Horrors*. In it, the heroine is a blonde bombshell from the wrong side of the tracks who dates a sadistic dentist who beats her up from time to time. She sings a song about her longing to leave the ghetto and find a home "Somewhere That's Green." It was very touching to me at that moment because I was having bad feelings about myself, and I could identify with her love for Seymour, who worked in the plant store with her, and her simultaneous feelings of unworthiness. The demon self-doubt lost a bit of its hold on me as I saw myself from a distance. I stepped aside a little as I listened to Audrey sing and could laugh and see myself through more compassionate eyes. There in the theater I was able to relax from the guilty fearfulness I'd been attacked by and, with my head on Tom's shoulder, enjoy the rest of the show.

I fell asleep on that same shoulder on the way back to Farmingdale on the train. We were really packing a lot of activity into one weekend. The next day was Sunday and church. Tom's belief that I, too, was an Italian Roman Catholic surfaced, and when I learned of these misconceptions I became upset. It soon melted away when I saw that Tom is not in the least bit dogmatic about his faith. He proved to be very open minded and interested in unorthodox belief systems. He, too, had experimented with self-help tapes, attempting to correct some problematic tendencies in his own life. What a relief it was to not be harshly judged by this one who was fast occupying a place in my heart!

This merely pointed out to me once again how perfectly God's plans work for us if we allow them to. Humans tend to think they need to manipulate circumstances in order to make them fit, when in reality it is merely a waste of time if we're being "led by the Spirit." Also, it tickles me when I remember the zealous scheming that helped to bring our meeting about. Tom's response when I broke the news to him of my true WASP identity was a deadpanned "Don't let the Godfather hear about this!" I was really beginning to love that man.

After church we headed into the city for more sightseeing. Stopping in a streetside deli, he playfully analyzed my handwriting (I am continually amazed at the scope of knowledge he accumulates) in efforts to figure me out and peer into my psyche a little bit deeper. We talked into the night over dinner and wine at the Stone Crab restaurant in Greenwich Village. I was on a soapbox as usual about something I had just heard about rock music and suicide, when he looked at me and said, "I love it that we're having these real conversations!" I learned that he loves a debate and is always well informed about nearly everything. Our minds were meeting, and a love affair was beginning.

Later, away from the noise and hectic rush of New York, back in my Midwestern home, I would allow myself the luxury of feeling the promise contained in those words: "Every meeting not a chance meeting, but planned by Me." Once again I would remember the prayer that danced through my mind for a soul to love, help, comfort, and bring joy to. For the moment we held hands and savored our final few hours together, unaware of the magnitude of what we were entering into.

All too soon midnight struck for this modern-day Cinderella, and I found myself boarding the plane on an early Monday morning flight back to St. Louis. The first weekend of October 1985 had come to an end, and my life would never again be the same. I smiled and calmly opened my dear little *God Calling* book as we prepared for take-off!

# 2

# *The Road Home*

> "The journey of a thousand miles starts with a single step." —Chinese Proverb

THE year 1985 brought many magical surprises, the highlight of which was the start of a romantic relationship that reinforced my faith in a God who intimately cares for my every need. Yet I am certain that it evolved as a direct result of the preparation period that shaped my mind and spirit in the years immediately preceding it, and that without them it could have been quite different. It is the small acts of obedience and love that accumulate to build wonderful results somewhere down the line, and it is only by slowly growing into the knowledge of who I am that I become a magnet that attracts others with the same ideals and aspirations. I wasn't ready for New York or Tom until I had had a few years of questing and had found some preliminary answers.

I attended high school in the late seventies, graduating in 1980, a time when values weren't easily defined. Around me was a smorgasbord of possibilities: Drugs and alcohol were everywhere, the pre-AIDS sexual "freedom" ethic was in full tilt, and an "If it feels good, do it" banner seemed to wave from the rafters. I was stumbling around pretty much like everyone else I knew, trying to make sense of my life. I joined a radical therapy group led by one of my English instructors and delved briefly into the world of "I'm O.K., You're O.K." philosophy. I learned better communication tools and how to be honest in relationships, but the sole focus was on the mind; spirit was ignored. I hadn't found what I was looking for.

Several years earlier a book had deeply affected me—cracked the door of my mind to new possibilities and, more important, a sense of purpose. My dad had passed it along to me with enthusiasm. At first I resisted the ideas it presented, but after devouring the book myself, I became convinced I had discovered one of very few pearls of great price. The ensuing years did not dull my positive impressions of that book, but it remained a part of my philosophy sadly removed from day-to-day life.

That eye-opening book was Gina Cerminara's *Many Mansions,* which chronicles the Edgar Cayce psychic readings' vision of the continuity of the soul. It brought sense to my theological misgivings and hope to my fearful heart. Cerminara painstakingly detailed the concept of reincarnation, the idea that the soul returns to earth to be reborn again and again in order to complete the lessons necessary for its return home. Having read the book, having been deeply moved by it, I would find it extremely difficult to settle for what I felt were only partial truths and half-baked theories.

I was in grade school when I embraced these new concepts, and it was difficult at that time to incorporate and blend my beliefs with traditional ones. I visited various churches, but couldn't get comfortable. I was in the stage of enthusiasm where I wanted to shout from the rooftops about the discoveries I was making and, while I loved my kitchen table talks with my dad, just discussing the theories and principles wasn't enough. I lacked the hot-blooded everyday implementation needed for them to come alive. So I shelved them for a while and experimented with other avenues of expression that brought people together, such as the radical therapy group. Still, I was at odds with myself, and I left high school feeling that my fire was only partially lit.

After graduation and a year spent floundering, I knew it was time to get serious about my life. I thought of *Many Mansions* and the urge to service it held. The readings had asked the question: "Is there really the desire to know love, or to know the experience of someone having an emotion over self? Is it a desire to be itself expended in doing that which may be helpful or constructive? This *can* be done, but it will require the *losing* of self, as has been indicated, *in* service for others." (1786-2)

I decided upon nurse's training as a way to get my hands and heart occupied with the business of serving others. I firmly believe that we can be helpful to others no matter what our profession is, but I felt at the time that bedside care of the sick was the right choice for me. So I set out to do just that.

During Christmas break that first year, 1981, I attended a party at the home of one of my fellow students. I was enjoying the warmth of good friends surrounding me, the beauty of the season with the lights and elaborate food, when suddenly I received a surprise blessing. I had walked into the kitchen to get more ice and was greeted by a quote taped to the refrigerator. Stopping to read, I almost dropped my glass—it was taken from the Cayce readings! Excitement shot through my body as I raced back to the living room to discover who the secret tape-wielding messenger was. I learned that my friend's mother was acquainted with the Cayce material, but not really involved in its study to a great extent. However, her best friend was attending a study group right there in our city. I took down her name and number and thus began my first membership in a Search for God study group. With that, my passion ignited.

Although I had had a taste of the Cayce philosophy, I was about to partake of an entire meal—complete with appetizers and dessert. I looked forward to Wednesday evenings as never before, when I would take my place in the living room with veterans of the material, to be introduced to and immersed in teachings so grand to my spirit that I truly felt I could not contain myself.

The study group books, *A Search for God,* Books I and II, were a result of a group of seekers who came together in February 1931 to study information given by Edgar Cayce in the trance state. The individuals did not progress to the next phase of subject matter in the readings until they had studied, practiced, and applied what was already given. One hundred thirty readings spanned eleven years and resulted in these two volumes written by the original members, screened and approved by the sleeping Cayce.

The first volume begins with a study of meditation. Page 2 states that "Meditation is not musing or daydreaming, but attuning our mental and physical bodies to their spiritual source . . . In prayer we speak to God, in meditation God speaks to us." I found that explanation beautifully succinct, and with the first few stones of spiritual practice laid, I was ready to begin my training.

The other two women in the group were the most vocal leaders, although each of us took turns at guiding the others through the weekly readings and prayers. Pam, the hostess who held the meetings in her home, reminded me of a teacher I had once had in grade school. She kept the conversation on track and always came prepared with complimentary reading material and well-thought-out comments related to the topic for the week. I admired her intelligence and well-cultivated manner.

Her husband, Samuel, brought down-to-earth, everyday examples from his own life to highlight the subject at hand. He was frequently quiet and tended to be a silent supporter of our endeavors.

Julia, the other woman in the group, was less precise than Pam, with a more relaxed style. Her strength lay in her well-tuned intuition. The two of them were just the examples I needed for bringing the concepts from the Edgar Cayce body of work into daily practice in my own life. Julia's husband, Don, added a touch of levity to our group with his weekly jokes and humorous insights.

Always following a discussion of the lesson, we would dim the lights, and each of us would assume a position of comfort with the spine straight in preparation for entering the silence. The Lord's Prayer recited aloud began the process of stilling the mind to hear God's voice. In order to remain on track, a short word or phrase spoken internally brought the focus back to the task at hand. It reminds me of the practice of reciting the rosary, with all thoughts laid aside and the words of the Lord's Prayer and Hail Mary in their place. In this way the quiet, still, small voice has an opportunity to speak once the recitation finishes and the mind is centered.

The purpose of meditation, as I see it, is to have communion with the Holy Spirit within us. Sometimes specific direction from other helpers is achieved as well. Julia received detailed instructions during her meditations. The advice she heard was generally earthy and practical, often concerned with survival techniques in the event of catastrophic earth changes, something predicted by Cayce as a potential happening in the 1990s. For instance, the advice might consist of how to refrigerate food underground or how to fashion a fishing hook—things our ancestors probably knew quite well. This knowledge is lost to many of us in twentieth-century America.

It was fascinating. We would crowd around a coffee table to munch wholesome snacks free of refined sugar (Pam had hypoglycemia) while listening to Julia detail what she had heard. Pam was the record keeper, carefully jotting down everything that was said. Occasionally, a personal message was relayed to one of us. For me it was once the urging to wear the color blue more often. I had never experienced anything like this before, and at first I was skeptical. Was this merely a figment of her imagination or an attention-getting device? Or perhaps angels were among us.

In time I observed enough of her to be aware of what the "fruits" of this practice were in her life, which is the gauge that Jesus gave His followers in determining how to discern whether or not prophecy is false. (Matthew 7:16) Witnessing her steady growth in kindness and wisdom put me at ease concerning the messages she relayed to us. Still, being barely out of my teen-age years, I found it difficult to have serious interest in the proposed earth changes that were yet a decade away.

My own initiation into the age-old practice of meditation was far less dramatic. I had no cosmic connections, no voices or visions. But I felt incredible peace when meditating with the others. It was bringing me in touch with that part of myself which remembers my inextricable connection to the Father. It was bringing me in touch with my soul.

My new friends guided me as we explored together "Co-operation," the first lesson in the wine-colored book. I learned that it is more than just working in unison with others, it is allowing the Divine to work through me. An essential part of our study was the setting of a weekly discipline to focus on during the interim. These were designed to help realign our thinking and acting; we were applying the knowledge just as the first study group had.

One of the most revealing disciplines from my standpoint was the week that we determined to refrain from criticism for seven days. It became clear to me that I needed to do a lot of work in order to curb that human tendency. While constructive criticism might be a helpful thing, by attempting to eliminate it altogether, my understanding was illuminated enough to realize that the vast majority of my detours into gossip and complaining are negative, plain and simple. Almost fifteen years later I'm still dealing with that one and realizing that it is a lifelong endeavor.

We moved through "Know Thyself" and on to "What Is My Ideal?"—the determining of which is an important step in growth. The readings state that by setting physical, mental, and spiritual ideals we make for ourselves patterns to follow in handling day-to-day decisions. For instance, my mental ideal is an attitude of joy and peace, and the physical ideals I've chosen that help me enact that are to smile often, speak kindly, and act in patience. These written guideposts help shape my actions and reactions. It isn't always easy to hold onto, but by affirming that—to have peace rather than conflict is my intent—the way unfolds.

The spiritual ideals form the basis for the others and encompass them as well. Simply put, mine is love. Love of the Father, love of the Son, love of my fellow humans and myself. In practice this means that whenever I'm confused, I can find the answer by looking to the ideal. Let's say that I'm angry at someone. The person has done something that I feel is an attack, and my defenses rise up to protect myself and "let 'em have it." I've struggled with this one many times. Part of me says, yes, your anger is justified, don't stuff it down or you'll only get ulcers. That is partially true. But if I'm being guided by my ideal of love, then blasting someone full force usually isn't the answer.

Love asks that I cool down, pray about it, then talk to the person I'm upset with. It takes more courage and self-control to wait until the high tide of rage is down and then sit down and discuss the real problem. It's easier to just "let 'em have it" in the height of passion or ignore it and seethe inside. Resentment can become a comfortable companion, difficult to say good-by to. The problem is that it eats away at us, literally, and many say that cancer is just one disease that is allowed a stronghold by this insidious monster.

Just as I was beginning to work with my ideals, an occasion arose to test what I would do about them. I was in the clinical phase of my nursing education, spending four hours a day working in a hospital nearby. Each morning I would report to the cafeteria at 6:30 to gather with the other students for coffee and breakfast before setting out for the nursing unit. We worked in groups of three or four, and I had been given an assignment with a woman who was beginning to irritate me. She seemed to look down her nose at everyone with a "holier-than-thou" attitude, and it really ticked me off. Each day it grated on me until I thought I couldn't stand it any more. One morning over coffee I unleashed some of my hostility in a gossipy, bitching session with the other students in our group.

I began to list the things I didn't like about her—her stuck-up attitude, her perfectionism and impatience with us younger students, on and on until suddenly the wind began to be knocked from me. I felt suddenly drained in the middle of my diatribe and realized that I was hurting not only myself but her. What was I learning in the weekly study group? That what we think and say about another person has an actual physical effect on them and us. Moreover, what about my ideals of love, peace, and speaking kindly? I felt heaviness of spirit all morning from the incident.

Later, when we were in our seats for afternoon classes, I tuned out the instructor as I thought of the woman about whom I had spoken harshly. I looked at her closely, and I felt myself beginning to melt. My internal wicked witch had been properly doused with water. I saw her as a struggling student, perhaps trying harder than she needed to due to her middle age and her returning to school after a long period of rearing children and taking care of a home. I prayed for help in releasing all the poisonous thoughts and words I'd had, asking that a blessing be their replacement. At home that night I wrote about the experience of confronting my own negativity and the realization that holding to an ideal really does effect change; I'd seen it in my own softened attitudes earlier in the day.

Working with her became easier, and either my perceptions changed or she actually became nicer. Sometimes we see what we expect to see, and our labeling of others causes us to focus on any action that reinforces our prejudice. Maybe I had been unaware of her gentleness all along. To this day when I slip into that type of slanderous talk, and I still can from time to time, I suffer tremendously afterward for it. I feel it almost immediately: the deep regret and strong self-loathing for acting in complete opposition to my own chosen, written ideals. Sometimes apologies are in order, and I need to climb down on my knees to wash the feet of the one I've insulted—even when the tongue lashing was only in my mind. It is only through an act of restitution, whether actual or imagined, along with prayer for forgiveness, that I am able to reclaim my peace of mind and self-respect.

Soon I graduated from nurse's training and took a private-duty position with a woman suffering from amyotrophic lateral sclerosis (ALS) or Lou Gehrig's disease. Just as in school where we had clinical assignments in addition to theory, I faced the opportunity of putting the attribute of patience, one of our study group book chapters, into practice in my new job. Another spiritual laboratory opened its doors.

ALS is a degenerative disease that attacks the nerves of the body, slowly producing muscle paralysis. In this case, my patient had already lost the ability to speak, walk, feed herself, or even apply her own make-up. She often couldn't make it to the bathroom in time and would have to have her clothes changed. She maintained a kind disposition despite all of this, though, and always offered me a smile when I came through her door.

It was difficult trying to decipher the sounds she would make when trying to communicate, and writing was extremely hard for her. I made a board with several of her most frequent needs printed on it, along with letters for her to point to and spell, but even that took strength that she was quickly losing. Many times she collapsed into tears when the total helplessness of her situation overwhelmed her.

My mother always had to urge me to be patient as a child, because I seemed to want everything to happen instantly. Now I was in a hospital room eight hours a day, painstakingly listening as she tried to communicate her needs to me. It was a challenge which I didn't always meet completely. Feeding time was lengthy, due to her swallowing impairment, and even though her food was puréed, she took at least a full hour to finish the tray. One night the trays were late for the third evening in a row. I waited and waited, getting more anxious by the minute because I had plans to go out later. Finally, tired of checking the hall to find nothing there, I told the nurses on duty that they would have to feed her since my shift had ended forty-five minutes earlier.

Now, technically, there was nothing wrong with this scenario. The hospital staff always took over my duties when I wasn't there, and they weren't shorthanded or exceptionally busy that night. Still, it ate away at me, and I carried the guilt for days. I felt that I hadn't met the situation in a spirit of patience, rather, in one of hurried annoyance. In the study group I had learned that patience is an attribute of the soul. Explained by author Mark Thurston, it is a dimension of measurement, along with time and space, that describes our experiences (*Experiments in a Search for God*, p. 73). Patience is the spirit in which we meet a situation!

A couple of years earlier I simply would have written off the incident as my overactive conscience putting me on a guilt trip, but I now knew that it was more. The realization for me was that becoming anxious and annoyed only worsens the situation. How much better I would have come away that day if I had either stayed a while longer, knowing that I wouldn't be late for my date; or in calmness asked the staff to take care of dinner for me. It was the spirit of rushing and getting restless that was in error. As always, though, there would be a next time when I could try again.

This assignment lasted only a few months and ended when she passed through death's door. I am thankful for the chance to experience her final days with her, and I hope that my prayers and presence were of some help, despite my novice understanding and application of my ideals. I know that I was certainly given an example and a model for my own growth in her loving quiescence and acceptance of her situation.

While my new-found awareness was urging me to take responsibility for my actions, at the same time the training was gentle. I began to see myself as a pilgrim on a journey and realized that Carolyn needed to be stricter yet kinder in dealing with her own shortcomings. Continual examination of faults is not what I learned; no, it was recognition of them followed by a plan of action and forgiveness of myself for falling short.

Along with study, prayer, and meditation, I began in my study group another practice essential to my spiritual health: dream interpretation. Weekly we would set aside time to talk through ours, and I started a daily log that was extremely detailed for many years. I will return to this in depth later, but for now I must say that it provided me with a method for gaining a greater connection with my true, but often hidden nature.

One of the most significant gifts that the group gave to me was an introduction to *God Calling*, the little book I carry with me, containing the words of Jesus spoken in recent times. It was vastly meaningful during my trip to New York, lending a touch of guidance that went beyond my ability to imagine. I fell immediately in love with the book the first time I heard Pam reading from it. It struck chords within me that I hadn't felt before, and I bought my own copy as soon as possible and have since had to replace worn-out volumes several times.

My spiritual body took in nourishment as weekly we met for our discussions, prayers, and meditation times. My resolve strengthened by linking with Pam, Samuel, Julia, and Don. They helped me see that it is the day-by-day tiny steps that we take in making our relationships with other people more loving that fashion our growth upward. It was with sadness that I left them when I graduated and moved away. It didn't take long to locate a new group, though, and once again I continued the greatest adventure I've ever known: that of the search for God.

Joining the study group was like finding a room at the top of the stairs, toward the end of the hall, that had been waiting with unlocked door forever. Entering brought discoveries of jewels, antique furnishings, and fine old volumes that merely needed to be dusted a bit and then explored. It brought sparkle, and comfort, and joy into life again. It brought me back to where I'd always been but didn't realize it—the road home—and traveling it became even more exciting as the journey continued.

# 3

# *The Beach*

> "Great nature has another thing to do to you and me; so take the lively air and lovely, learn by going where to go." —Theodore Roethke

TIMES of retreat are essential to keeping the mind, body, and spirit renewed. If partaken with the accompaniment of ocean breeze or mountain stream, it is all the better. My activity in the study group sparked a desire in me to visit the A.R.E. headquarters and receive a dose of the mystic adrenaline that had already begun to pump throughout my soul. I went seeking the kind of inspiration that makes it possible to live life differently, with a sense of expectation and a belief that anything is possible.

While between jobs in 1982—my first year out of nursing school—my number-one priority was making the trip to

Virginia Beach; the hunt for work would wait. The study group had heaped coals upon my inner fire, and it was burning more brightly than ever. My growth was happening so naturally through the tools the group made available that I was eager to spend more than just an evening at a time exploring them. I phoned the A.R.E. to find out if any conferences were happening at that time of the year and was thrilled to hear of the 1983 New Year's gathering set to begin after Christmas. Since all of the airlines were either booked solid or too expensive, I settled on a Greyhound bus to lead me to my destination. I began preparing for the twenty-four-hour trip from Illinois to Virginia.

Making the trip to the A.R.E. headquarters was an important milestone for me. What did I expect to find when I got there? A greater sense of what the work of the Association was all about and of my being a part of it. The readings had changed my life entirely: They helped to resuscitate my relationship with Jesus Christ, nudged me to explore the wealth of guidance available within myself, and presented me with detailed concepts with which to work. I felt excited about life on earth and the life beyond. It was a kind of pilgrimage for me to travel to the place where much of the activity of this sort centered. I was not disappointed.

I settled in once the long ride was over, then headed to the main auditorium for registration and orientation. After the welcoming speech, I returned to my hotel room to mull over the list of workshops available to me. There was much to choose from and so many new feelings for me to experience. The camaraderie of the others who shared my deep interest in matters of spirit, the thrill of knowing that this was where so much of the original "action" had taken place, the majesty of the former Cayce hospital perched atop the hill. The latter now held offices, but at one time it was a haven of dreams—dreams of treating the sick according to the readings' advice, of testing their validity and applicability in an objective fashion by doctors and nurses who wished to blaze a new trail. The crash of the stock market and the ensuing Depression had forced its doors to close. The white building still stood proudly, though, eager to house those who continued to make the wheels turn in this growing organization of seekers.

A feeling of peace seemed to drift through the salty sea air, perhaps due to decades of prayers raised by the pilgrims drawn to this work. Hearing the speakers whose books I had read and studied simply added the crowning touch. My introduction that week to the headquarters of this work was reflective and thought provoking. I had seven days away from all responsibility and familiarity to explore within myself more deeply. The foundation that the study group had laid was perfect for the added construction and completion of sublime ideas.

I returned seven months later, already hungry for more, to attend the "Love Is Letting Go of Fear" conference. Again I was met with the overall feeling of "coming home," a quiet, centering experience at times, heart-racing excitement at others. This time I also found something more.

Enter George: Holographer/Juggler/Writer/Engineer/Artist/Seeker/ Forever Friend . . . Extraordinaire!

The three Milwaukee brothers—George, Jerry, and Dick—attended the conference and stayed at the wonderful old Marshall's Hotel, same as me. Jerry, handsome and tanned, was romancing one of my assigned roommates, and thus we all became fast friends.

This particular conference week focused on the *Course in Miracles* material. Well-known author Gerald Jampolsky was the featured speaker, and the conference was of the same title as his best-selling book, *Love Is Letting Go of Fear.* I chose this particular conference because of an introduction to the concepts the *Course* teaches during an afternoon workshop given by Dr. Kenneth Wapnick at the New Year's assembly. I didn't fully grasp the meaning of the teaching at that time, but became intrigued. This week devoted itself to the principles, and I came hoping to learn more. My mind and spirit felt especially stirred by the rediscovered friendships surrounding me.

Soon after our arrival, the Milwaukee brothers gathered at the hotel with my roommate and me before dinner. Then it was on to Gus's Fish House for a feast. It was like listening to an episode of MASH as the three brothers teased back and forth. Their personalities were so different, and yet they shared a common thread of humor and understated sarcasm. I loved every minute of it.

Jerry was quiet and kind; brother Dick, laid back and lovable; George, always full of fire and ire over the ideas that seemed to be bursting from him. I can be uncomfortable sometimes with new people, due to the shyness I've been battling all of my life, but there was instant rapport and complete ease during our relaxed meal. We had seats overlooking the ocean, and the magnificent backdrop no doubt added to the effortlessness I felt. I found myself admiring their bond with one another. Three brothers, all with grown children of their own, having a good time together, creating memories to last forever. Now I was a part of their circle. A big smile crept over me. Minds, hearts, and stomachs full, we made our way to the auditorium for the evening lecture; then to the Marshall's Hotel for a late night walk on the beach.

I have spoken to others who agree that these star-filled nights overlooking the ocean are quite conducive to opening the heart and mind to true communication and friendship. I have to agree. Back in the Oceanscope Room, the late-night Marshall's gathering place, we settled into the comfortable sofa. George made me laugh even when he didn't mean to be funny. Intellectual, with a mind always reaching for the absurd and often overlooked, the two of us had a lot to discuss.

He had been coming to the Beach for three years, a strong enthusiast of the readings and a lover of ocean breezes. Divorced, with two sons around my age, he began his spiritual search some time after the breakup of his marriage. Funny, I thought, how agonizing circumstances can often be the impetus for transformation. When the lights go out in one area of life, suddenly there's a lot of time and space to stop for a moment and consider where we're going as we scramble to find a candle. Illness can do it, death, divorce—all of these poke us in the eye and force confrontation with what's inside us. George and I talked past midnight.

Morning comes awfully soon after a late night spent catching up with friends. I was never able to arouse myself early enough to participate in the 7:00 a.m. exercise sessions on the beach, which are led by A.R.E. staff. Yet I would manage to be awake, showered, and ready for a breakfast sharing group on time. Sharing groups meet each day for breakfast and lunch to talk, experiment, and get to know one another. The Oceanscope Room at the rear of the hotel streamed with light from the morning sun; and, with the sound of the waves in the background, it was easy to enter a heightened state of awareness.

One morning while nibbling toast and eggs, as group members shared tidbits from dreams they'd had the night before, I began to feel a sense of timelessness creeping into the room. Suddenly, in the midst of voices and laughter I seemed to be a part of, yet apart from, the group. I drank in the moment, feeling its temporary permanence. I instantly knew what the phrase "time stood still" means, as I savored the wonderful realization of how joyous it was to be alive! In a flash the sensation disappeared, as we cleared our table to make the 9:00 a.m. lecture. But I still remember.

That room; that warm, inviting "have a seat in Grandma's house" room was becoming a focal point for my days and nights. Between lectures, during meals, over drinks and celebrations late at night, I would be drawn again and again into its arms. The old Cape Cod feeling in the decor held secrets I wanted to uncover. A huge piano sat in the corner, poised and ready for nimble fingers to bring it once more to life. Lounge-chair sofas with large yellow-flowered cushions lined the perimeters, additional chairs interspersed between them allowed for separate groups to form. A white-brick fireplace faced all visitors when they entered.

Occasionally someone with a guitar would join the group and create the ambience of late-night campfire singing. Always the huge windows that overlooked the Atlantic Ocean made for a scene undeniably irresistible in its grandeur. Baked into the walls by sun and sea salt were the unmistakable effects of the presence of many, many fellow journeyers who had graced those chairs and sofas and filled the air with talk and prayer.

Feelings of stress and worry evaporated as I sensed the uplifting sensations in that room. This is what I had come for, a further arousal of my potential to feel love rather than fear. To lay aside guilt, self-condemnation, and any and all other hang-ups I might have allowed myself to accumulate over the years. To become refreshed and full of the knowledge of the Light within myself and others, and return to the core of what is truly important while we are here on this planet—to demonstrate love.

Each night I would walk across the street to the conference hall to hear the powerful ideas that I'd been enticed to learn on my first trip months earlier. Author of the book that shared its name with our conference title, "Love Is Letting Go of Fear," Dr. Gerald Jampolsky spoke to us one evening. A psychiatrist who founded the Center for Attitudinal Healing in California, Jampolsky is dedicated to helping the catastrophically ill cope with their illness by changing their mind-sets. He explained that, according to the *Course in Miracles,* whose tenets his organization is founded on, peace of mind is the single goal. That sounded simple to me. I remembered Jesus' message to His followers that He came to give peace—not the peace of the world, but the peace which passes understanding.

The world would probably identify peace of mind as having a "piece of the rock" or financial security. Money in the bank, good health, and well-adjusted kids. But Jesus (who is also believed by some to be the author of the *Course*) didn't say that. He only assured us of a harmony within our minds, not necessarily of outer circumstances. I longed to really depend fully on that truth in my own life, to live every day with the knowledge that all is well.

Dr. Jampolsky continued to speak about the need to live in the moment, instead of in constant fear of the terrible past and the uncertain future. Again I reflected on Jesus' words in the Lord's Prayer, "Give us this day our daily bread," showing us how important it is to stay focused on the immediate present. I was soaking up the principles that I needed to carry on. Afterward, a long walk on the beach with my friends brought a fitting close to the day—laughter, the roar of the ocean, and a black sky that seemed to lend an atmosphere of mystery.

The experience I was having was like dining out at a sumptuous buffet. The wonderful gourmet meal wouldn't contain even a tiny portion of the enjoyment and satisfaction if not shared with those I love. Most likely it would also fade fast from memory if not colored by traces of shared feelings and ideas. Jesus said that we get to heaven leaning on the arm of another, and that is what it is all about. George, Jerry, and Dick were becoming as close to me as any brothers could be, with our friendship engraved in time. Learning among friends was far superior to solitary musing, at least for me. The readings said it beautifully, "Be the *best* of whatever position thou doth occupy; as a wife, the best *wife* in the whole community; as a friend, the *best* friend; and there is the friend that sticketh closer than the brother; yea, the friend that gives rather his life for a friend. Ever gave ye the truths that thine brother might enjoy even a moment's rest in the Lord?" (262-29)

It had become clear to me why the trip to Virginia Beach was so important. The work of the A.R.E. was one aspect of my pull to go there, but just as strong was the need to once again find and unite with my counterparts whom I had no doubt known long ago. And to experience a place that reinforced my desire to serve God, a place that felt like home away from home.

Just before catching the plane that would take me back to Illinois, back to the reality of everyday work and play, I lay on the beach listening to the surf one more time. The warm white sand had a naturally tranquilizing effect upon me as I stared at the waves doing their repetitive dance. My mind cleared, and I drifted into that special, secret place where words aren't necessary and for a few moments I knew. I knew that all my fears were groundless and that I am loved much more than my mind can grasp. True renewal had found me there, and I touched the mystery.

A little breath of heaven found me in a seaside town and made it easier for me to breathe it in wherever I am. I could go back to my Midwestern home refreshed, to my new hospital position that I'd recently taken, my first since my 1982 graduation. I was ready.

# 4

# *Beyond Convention*

> "There are more things in heaven and earth, Horatio, than are dreamt of in your philosophy."
> —Shakespeare's Hamlet

I chose to become a nurse after answering the call to service that echoed to me from the Cayce readings. I began as a nursing assistant, getting my feet wet in order to determine if I could really care for others' physical needs. I followed that by becoming a licensed practical nurse; I wanted to begin working in as short a time as possible, and I had visions of becoming a poet and songwriter and that would require having plenty of spare time to devote to these dreams. Along the way I decided to continue with school after all, while privately maintaining my writing, and I became a registered nurse.

The readings were not only a guide for my career path, but a resource for expanding it as well. After all, they are full of information about care of the body and physical healing. I've massaged my own sore joints many times with peanut oil, and castor oil packs to my abdomen helped relieve a chronic skin condition. These are but two of the most well known of the Cayce "remedies"; the list goes on and on.

The question was, how could I fully incorporate the philosophy of treating the whole person that Cayce's work inspired into my role as a nurse? The foundation for my professional life as a holistic health practitioner was laid when I found my mentor, Virginia C. My first night on the third floor surgical unit with her, four months out of nursing school, was a welcome surprise.

I was homesick for the Search for God study group I had left when I graduated and moved to another city and thought that my studies would probably be solitary for a while. This thirty-year veteran R.N. greeted me by handing me a policies book to glance at and, as she walked away, asking when my birthday was. When I told her, she replied, "Great, an Aquarian! We've got enough Pisces running around this place," and threw another nurse a playful smile. I thought, "Wow, this is unusual; a boss who is open to the metaphysical world." Angels were surely watching over me!

Tall and imposing, with her long hair pulled back in a bun, Virginia looked much scarier than she was. The 11:00 p.m. to 7:00 a.m. shift was a pleasure when she was there. When it was slow, we found plenty to talk about, and she taught all of us novices a thing or two about being a good nurse. One bit of advice that has always stayed with me was the need to listen to an inner nudge. "Even if you've just made rounds and were in a patient's room moments earlier, don't ignore the draw to go back," she counseled and went on to illustrate her point by relating a couple of the times when she had done just that and prevented a man from hanging himself and intervened just as a patient was entering cardiac arrest. Hers was a finely tuned intuitive ability, which probably resulted from many years of paying attention to those urges.

God's hand was clearly involved in my landing this, my first hospital position. Virginia and some of the others had an interest in the Cayce material; she had read a few books concerning his work many years ago. We could explore together. Many times we prayed for patients or helped one another figure out a dream. Then we decided to begin working with Therapeutic Touch, as described by Dolores Krieger, Ph.D., R.N., in her book *The Therapeutic Touch: How to Use Your Hands to Help or to Heal*.

According to Krieger, Therapeutic Touch is especially useful in relaxing the patient and relieving pain. Virginia and I worked on a surgical unit, caring for people preparing for and recovering from such painful and anxiety-provoking procedures as gall bladder and hemorrhoid removal (these were the pre-laser surgery years). We had a perfect testing ground for touch therapy. First, we would need to absorb as much theory concerning this unusual intervention as possible.

The basic premise is that the practitioner is not "healing" the person, but simply directing energy either away from or toward trouble areas to bring about balance in another person's energy field. Krieger taught this innovative, yet age-old practice to nursing students in a master's level program at the University of New York in a program entitled Frontiers in Nursing. At least eighty other colleges and universities across the country now include it in their curriculum. Since 1979 when her first book was published, there have been numerous scientific studies validating the effects of this treatment, and it has gained widespread acceptance in the professional nursing arena.

This type of therapy requires a clear and centered mind,

a meditative state of concentration. My time spent in the study group would prove useful in achieving this. Before beginning, we practiced at the nurse's station with each other. In order to sense the energy field around us, we first placed our palms together, using a rubbing motion, then slowly moved them apart, while feeling the warm energy flow between them. Next, we experimented with feeling that same energy around one another's bodies, as we felt for changes in the pattern, such as cold, heat, pulling, or tingling, all of which might signify problem areas.

One morning after a night off, Virginia and I decided to visit a nurse nearby who had her own practice utilizing Therapeutic Touch. Up to that time we had had some promising results during our experimentation, but we wanted to learn from someone more skilled in the application.

The office was small, nonassuming, and its owner made us feel right at home as she led us to one of her tiny examination rooms equipped with comfortable but sparse furniture. The lights dimmed, and I relaxed in the straight-backed chair as the process began. With palms open, she scanned my body like radar, detecting any areas of potential discomfort. When she reached the area of my neck—a place often troubled by a nagging ache—I felt extreme heat. It was vibrating throughout my shoulders as she directed it away from my cervical spine.

Any skepticism I may have harbored drained away along with the soreness of my neck muscles. I left her office a more firm believer in the power of touch (although the hands don't actually meet the skin's surface; rather, they are approximately an inch from it). The pain had left me, and now I was able to sense energy fields much more acutely than before. With a block in my awareness removed, I could now accelerate the learning process. Virginia felt the same way. We returned to our jobs enthusiastic about the breakthrough we had made together.

As my poetry writing during that time reflects, these were years of badly needed grounding, as I lived an almost hermit-like existence. My world revolved around the study group, work, sleep, and quiet time. My social life nearly grinded to a halt while I worked the night shift, but it was as if a magical private universe opened up when I stepped off the third floor elevator each night at 10:30. It was a sacred time in my life.

Night after night in the velvet darkness softened only by the dim bedside light, Virginia and I practiced our newfound nursing skill. We would explain to our patients that what we were doing was merely using the energy field that surrounds everyone's bodies to direct energy toward or away from painful areas. While both of us felt there was a deeper spiritual significance and that the power of love was a major factor in what we were doing, we kept it as simple as possible in order to gain acceptance from those we wished to help. No one refused our interventions; some even continued the process in our absence.

Once, I began my rounds to find a middle-aged postoperative patient in the throes of intense pain. The intramuscular Demerol® I'd given him helped some, but still he moaned in agony. The anesthesia had left him in a rather confused state of mind, which can be a normal side effect, but I gave my explanation anyway and proceeded to use my hands to try to help. He stared up at me with big eyes, seemingly fascinated by what he was feeling. Before long, his muscles relaxed and we were able to turn him to another position in bed, a measure essential in a surgical patient's recovery. When I checked on him again, he was asleep.

The following night I was off work, but when I returned a day later my co-workers had an interesting report to give me. It seems that they entered the patient's room and found him asking where the "voodoo girl" was, using his own hands above the surgical site while muttering "dddddddd ... dddddddd ... dddddd" in fast progression, mimicking a vibration. We had a quite a laugh over that one, but I think a few people became believers that night.

Virginia and I continued to learn and practice nursing together for over a year, and then she moved on to become a hospice nurse, helping dying patients make their exit in dignity, surrounded by love. Cancer patients often suffer excruciating pain, making her skills in touch therapy a godsend. She's an amazing woman and a true channel of blessings. I continued without her, but always with the spirit of her helpfulness guiding me.

I maintained my practice in the art of healing touch both at work and at home. I explored it with my four tiny nephews, and they were in awe at the sensations it brought. Jeff's two-year-old tummy hurt one day, and I laid him, clothed only in a diaper, on the floor of his living room and went to work. He smiled and seemed amused by the warm, slightly charged feeling produced when I held my hands an inch from his abdomen, and relief soon came. I also used the laboratory of my home to try the techniques with baby Jason and found it useful when he was particularly fussy, despite all the usual interventions of diaper change, bottle, and rocking.

As emphasized in the Cayce material, all healing, all energy, is from the One Source, God. We're just helpers, facilitating that force to flow to others. Many years after my work with Therapeutic Touch, I crossed paths with someone who presented a wide range of information that expanded my repertoire in this fascinating field of "energy medicine," as it is known. I had managed to overlook a segment of research that the readings had spurred, but this new friend brought it to my attention through his passionate zeal for making it well known and available to the public.

Bruce Baar, a Philadelphia medical-sales professional,

uses time and talents to develop and market specialized devices purportedly used for balancing the energies within the body, devices outlined in the readings and suggested for a multitude of disorders. And he does this on his own time, using his own cash. It was for people like him that the word "dedication" was coined.

These innovative devices were suggested most often for increasing the circulation and to normalize functioning of the nervous system. Two of them are the wet-cell appliance or Regeneron™ and the impedance device, also known as the Radiac™ (trademark names instituted by Bruce).

A reading given concerning these devices said this, "The vibrations... aid in producing that vibration necessary, not only for the coordination of the glandular system but for the ability in the nerve itself to be rejuvenated... this works directly upon the glandular system; the thyroid, the adrenals and the thymus, *all* the glands of the body; thus enabling them to react as assimilating forces. For that is the process or the activity of the glands, to secrete that which enables the body, physically, throughout, to *reproduce* itself!" (1475-1)

I met Bruce in Virginia Beach during Congress week at the A.R.E., a time when members from around the world gather to celebrate and become more deeply involved in the organization's grass-roots operations. He gave lectures on the devices and offered his assistance to people interested in experimenting with their use at home. We immediately became good friends, bonded by a common love for the readings. Clearly, he is gifted in being able to explain complicated ideas so that they become simple and easy to comprehend. I learned in conversations with him that it was his own trouble with allergies and asthma that drove him to try the devices for himself. He was very young at the time and indeed found relief through the application.

The mainstream medical profession is seeing the rise of

energy medicine as a phenomenal source of help. Electricity in medicine goes back to Aristotle's time when electric eels, rays, and catfish produced numbness in patients. Such things as TENS units (transcutaneous electrical nerve stimulation), iontophoresis, functional electrical stimulation, and shortwave diathermy are all examples of modern medicine's advances in using the interaction of electricity with the body to produce everything from pain relief to movement of paralyzed limbs. Functional electrical stimulation uses electrodes to stimulate muscles of the body that have been dysfunctional, as in the case of spinal cord injury and resultant paralysis. We are now witnessing how marvelous breakthroughs, such as these, change what was once a dim prognosis into something more hopeful.

While the idea for the wet-cell appliance and impedance device came from a person in a trance state, this is no reason for the medical world to turn its attention away from this potential. What Cayce did was simply tap into knowledge in a way that is different from ordinary waking thought, yet not so different from the scientists' methods of discovering potential breakthroughs. How many leaders in our history have developed ground-breaking technology with the help of their subconscious minds in the dream state? Perhaps one day what Cayce did will be looked upon as an acceptable act of "tuning in" to the infinite intelligence. Until then, prejudice aside, we must test the applicability of what he gave. Bruce has joined with the many health-care providers, researchers, and consumers in a quest for establishing their usefulness. In the meantime, we all have access to the most basic energy conduit—our hands.

After three years, I left my third-floor beginnings armed with the best of post-textbook instruction and experience. Always seeking variety and challenge, I held a series of independent contracting positions that ran the gamut of clinical settings. From pediatric high-tech home care to nursing home charge nurse, I dove into my responsibilities with my eyes open for new ways to ease burdens and be a light to others in whatever way God allowed me.

Virginia would have loved to see the ingenuity (sparked by her example) that I took with me into the home of a woman bedridden and attached to a respirator. And she would smile to hear of the lessons in living that I was given in the process.

Harriet was spending her last days in a small bedroom, unable to breathe for herself or even speak—the tracheostomy tube made that an impossibility. She wrote out her requests on paper, and mostly slept and fought our attempts to move her. The bland depressiveness of her surroundings hit me like a cold chunk of cement—gray, hard, and chilling. As is common of those with chronic obstructive pulmonary disease, Harriet kept her thermostat so low that we nurses had to wear sweaters and sit on a heating pad to keep warm, despite the fact that it was a burning ninety-five degrees outside! It was truly tomb-like.

There was no television in her room. No books to keep her mind occupied or music to still her soul. I saw before me a woman in waiting, waiting for death to remove her from her bodily prison. I could not simply sit by and wait with her; I had to at least try to stir her one more time before her exit.

Along with Therapeutic Touch, I incorporated some other types of stimulus to break through to her. Since there were no pictures on the walls, I decided to make of myself a painting. Antiseptic whites went the way of the hamper, and I dug through my closets for every bright shirt I owned. I began to report to her home at 6:30 a.m. in vivid greens, blues, and fuchsias. If she noticed, she didn't say.

I also determined that light piano music might brighten her mood, so I toted my tape recorder into her room and mentioned that I wanted her to listen along with me. In little time she asked me to turn it off. It seemed that Harriet had already shut down and didn't want to be awakened, at least not yet. I had to respect that decision.

One day I reported to work and she was glowing. Knowing that I was open to the spiritual dimension, she shared with me a dream she'd had the night before. Babies, angelic-looking babies, had surrounded her in the dream. They left her with a happiness that I hadn't seen in her. That day she gave me a picture taken of herself in her younger days, standing in a light blue pantsuit next to a Christmas tree. I knew that she'd been moved, and I smiled with her, thankful for His mysterious ways.

It wasn't long after that that Harriet was released from this lifetime. She died during the night. I wasn't there, but she stopped to say good-by anyway. I was dreaming of her. She was in a huge, bright kitchen filled with food and loving family. Her excited, beaming words to me were, "Don't you love my new house?" Yes, Harriet, I love your new house, and I know that color and sound and laughter have come alive for you there once more. Save a place at the table for me, my friend.

When we hear the call, we never can really be sure just where it will lead us. We can be assured that stepping out into a life of service is as exciting as it gets—and that the appropriate helpers will be there all along the way to guide, encourage, and be examples of how the true servant lives and dies.

# 5

## Star Crossed

> "Let there be spaces in your togetherness."
> —Kahlil Gibran

A profession in nursing provided direction and helped me in my early attempts at living with a sense of purpose and mission. I was three years into my career when through prayer and patience I met Tom. My cross-country blind date seemed part of a natural progression to me at the time. One blessing of youth is that we usually feel a positive conviction about the possibilities contained in our own lives. Feelings of awe are accompanied by a natural faith in the belief that miracles are supposed to happen to us. God's incredible directing power brought us together and helped us live out our first year together. That was easy. The hard part was trusting in His sovereignty when the road took an uphill turn.

Frequent flier miles skyrocketed after our meeting, along with our long-distance phone bill. In November, Tom made his first trip to Springfield to visit me. He stayed with Taras, who lived close by in another apartment complex. I planned a party to introduce him to my friends and a trip to nearby Nauvoo, Illinois, a Mormon settlement town on the border of Iowa that a friend had enthusiastically recommended.

It was late the day we left for Nauvoo, and the sun was already beginning to set. We drove through hills and next to cornfields in my little red Datsun B210, enjoying easy conversation and laughter. Our spur-of-the-moment decision to leave so late meant that it was dark by the time we reached our destination—the sites we had come to see were closed until morning. We found a room in an old-fashioned area of town, near the Mormon village. Neither of us had brought along clothes or toiletries, so a trip to the local drugstore for toothpaste was in order.

Still slightly shy with one another, we drove into Iowa for dinner before heading back to our room. Once there I self-consciously prepared for bed, then we kissed goodnight and slipped into sleep. The next morning was cloudless and bright. Despite feeling rumpled from sleeping in the blue sweater and jeans that I'd worn the day before, day two in that outfit was wonderful just the same.

After breakfast we visited the community that the Mormons had once settled in on their journey westward. The history of the town engrossed us for the next several hours. Joseph Smith, founder of the sect, had changed the town's name from Commerce to Nauvoo. His vision of golden plates that urged him to create a new church of latter-day saints had meant that much of his life was spent in persecution by others outside his religion. His life ended on June 27, 1844, when he was arrested and shot in jail.

A model of the Mormon temple sits in the center of a courtyard, in front of large concrete tablets describing the city of Nauvoo and the place of worship. The restored shops and houses gave us a glimpse of early Mormon life. The print shop, pottery house, drugstore, and bakery provided background on the disciplined life style of the early religious devotees.

Absorbing an atmosphere of faith by discovering some of our country's religious cornerstones was inspiring to Tom and me. From the cathedrals we'd visited in New York City on our first date to this simple little town, we explored the paths of others motivated by the desire to find and serve God. This unlikely tourist spot was a highlight of his first visit to my corner of the world.

Back in Springfield, I made arrangements to bring Tom home with me to Decatur for dinner with my mom and dad. My stomach was all fireflies, fluttering and tingling at regular intervals. We arrived after dark, and though it was a cold night, that didn't stop my mom from weathering the great outdoors to cook steaks on her gas grill. A fantastic cook, she outdid herself as usual. Her labors produced a huge salad, baked potatoes, and tender juicy T-bones with which to woo her daughter's new beau.

I soon realized that I needn't have been so nervous. Tom and my parents talked as though they'd known each other forever. Their shared vitamin enthusiasm caused Tom and my mom to take off in discussion. After dinner, my three-year-old nephew Jeff went along on a drive to search out Christmas lights with his aunt and her curious new friend. He erupted in squeals of laughter as Tom entertained him with his unique brand of humor. Over and over Jeff would say, "You're siwy (silly), siwy, siwy, Tom!" His first step into my family's domain went well.

The following month, December, I flew to New York once more to attend the wedding of a close college friend of

Tom's. I discovered a deep contrast between the simple, down-to-earth ham sandwich buffets that usually constituted a grand wedding reception in central Illinois and the opulent hors d'oeuvre and prime rib sit-down dinners of a Northeastern ho-down! I appreciate the merits of both.

I could see that my new man was well loved by his buddies and a wonderful conversationalist in social situations. I was proud to be at his side. We danced, ate the delicious meal, and grew a little closer still.

In February Tom again visited the Midwest. This time I introduced him to Mark Twain country—Hannibal, Missouri. We toured two turn-of-the century mansions, the Mark Twain museum, and an underground cave common to the Missouri landscape. Back in Springfield, he enrolled in the advanced cardiac life support course that the medical school offered. It warmed me when he said that he wished he'd had me beside him during medical school.

On Valentine's Day, 1986, his course was completed, and we spent a romantic evening at the movies, then back at my apartment listening to music and watching television. I brought out a large platter of fresh vegetables, dip, cheese, and crackers. We opened a bottle of Chablis and toasted his success in the ACLS course. Then he turned to me and whispered, "I love you." I was glad he said it first. The day was flawless, and I considered it my first "real" Valentine's celebration.

We were having the time of our lives, but we were still in the honeymoon phase of our relationship. Each time we met was filled with new sites, quiet dinners, and the thrill of expectation that is inherent in a long-distance romance. When we were apart, we spent hours on the telephone. When we were together, we knew that our time was limited and that made it all the more sweet. In order to pass the true litmus test of compatibility, we knew we would have to take up residence in the same city.

Springtime erupted in brilliant color, a romantic time of

the year. It also brought plans for a new beginning for Tom and me. Bethlehem, Pennsylvania, had called us to its hills. With plans for completing additional training at the hospital there, Tom prepared to settle in in May, then come to Illinois to help me move. We loaded my car with high hopes and basic necessities, then set out for our great adventure.

Our first summer together started out well. I found an apartment two blocks away from Tom's, a furnished second story with a view. It was one hundred years old, full of history and high ceilings. The windows were bordered in stained glass, with a small balcony off the living room. I loved it. I spent hours there writing poetry and, when fall arrived, studying for the full-time classes for which I'd signed up.

I found a Search for God study group in nearby Allentown and joined this group of four older women who had been meeting for several years. It was a good spiritual touchstone for me to have in this new, strange town.

Bethlehem had been settled by the Moravians, a Christian sect who had come to the area seeking religious freedom. The founder of the denomination, John Huss, is considered the forerunner of the Protestant Reformation. In fifteenth-century Czechoslovakia, Huss felt that the Catholic church was becoming too worldly and full of abuses. He sought a return to a simple faith based on the Bible and the early followers of Jesus. He was denounced by the church and labeled a heretic. For his words of revolution he was burned at the stake in 1415, an event which started a civil war in Moravia.

Breaking with tradition had carried a heavy price for these brave believers. John Huss's call to practice the basic tenets that Jesus taught didn't die with him. Our new city still housed those who attempted to carry on with his conviction. Bethlehem maintained the old world charm of the nineteenth century, with cobblestone streets and historic buildings dotting the countryside. A large star on top of one of its hills is lit at night to signal to travelers that they've reached the namesake of the birthplace of Jesus.

Soon after moving there, I found myself alone more and more often. Tom had to spend long hours at the hospital, and I sometimes only saw him during a quick dinner break. My love of solitary time was really stretched to its limit. Fortunately, I found work easily with a nearby nursing agency and became particularly attached to one of the home-care cases they assigned me with a young quadriplegic injured during a drag race a couple of years earlier. But work ended after eight hours, and I returned to a lonely place.

Our easy beginnings were transforming into difficult times. Tom's favorite grandfather became ill in September and died suddenly. The grief surrounding his death, coupled with the stress of learning the ropes as a young physician, made day-to-day life hard for Tom. I began to see another side of him. That of a strong fighter who doesn't give up. I was glad to be able to share his doubts and heartaches with him and to witness him survive when the pressure was on.

We were standing up to the test, and though we disagreed and fought from time to time, we always seemed able to talk through the rough spots. I felt confident that the next logical step was a permanent commitment.

Christmas came, and I flew home to visit my family. He drove me to the airport and left me with a kiss and a promise of exchanging gifts when I returned. I was beginning to sense that Tom and I might not be on the same wavelength when it came to the value of vows. There was no holiday proposal, but I still had hopes for our second Valentine's Day. When that passed without so much as a mention of wedding bells, I suspected that I was dealing with nuptial phobia. The only solution in my mind was for me to broach the subject.

Ah, the ability of the marriage-timid to dance around that fearful topic! I never heard him actually admit to being hesitant. Instead, he insisted that it was what he wanted, too, yet could never be pinned down to a specific time frame. By April I was becoming angry at being led on by his indecision. July would bring an internship in Baltimore, and I didn't want to move again if he couldn't come to a firm decision.

He remained deeply planted in ambiguity. The natural progression that we had flowed with until now had hit a pothole. If we couldn't move forward, then we either had to stay stuck in the mire or back up. I decided to turn back. I made plans to return to Illinois and provide some space and time for both of us to evaluate where we wanted to be in our lives together.

Only ten months earlier we had set out together, now we were preparing to part. I helped him move to Baltimore, and he continued to try to persuade me to stay.

I made cream-colored curtains for his apartment, arranged the kitchen, and prayed for God's direction. It was tempting to remain there with him, but I felt that in the long run staying true to the decision I'd made was essential. A perpetual dating arrangement, something I had witnessed in other couples, was not what I wanted.

Leaving was painful. We drove back to Illinois together, sad and unsure when we would see one another again. Bethlehem was a dim star quickly fading in the background.

Fortunately, I didn't possess a working crystal ball. If I had seen the troubled times that we would face together, the painful separations and breakups, I don't know if I'd have stayed for the happy ending. I was protected by my lack of omniscience as I went on with my life. I returned to Decatur, and my interest in spiritual studies went forward. I was flooded with new friends who shared that passion.

But in our relationship, we had entered the Egypt of our

experience—a time of separation and questioning. We had left Bethlehem with our love not fully matured, yet no longer in its infancy. The amazing power of our Father continued to smooth the rough spots for us. A year later, in remarkable fashion, Tom would start a residency in St. Louis, a mere 120 miles from my home. That move would bring surprises and heartaches as well as eventual joy. For the moment I doubled up on the spiritual disciplines that had kept me moving through life inspired. With the Master designer still in charge, my molding process continued.

# 6

## First a Dream

> "And the angel of God spake unto me in a dream..."  —Genesis 31:11

"AN uninterpreted dream is like an unopened letter," an intriguing observation espoused by the Talmud I've heard quoted along the way. Sometimes those "letters" are like news from home, leaving me with a familiar happiness. Other times they more closely resemble hate mail as I try to unscramble dark images and fearful feelings. Then in the midst of wondering if all of these messages are really meaningful, there comes the dream that reaffirms the belief that something magical is truly happening as we close our eyes and slip into sleep.

When I awoke that morning, twenty-something years

ago, I was in a daze. My mind was not on my oatmeal as I tried to savor the feelings I'd just experienced; it was lost somewhere in theta waves, searching for the man of my dreams. His name was Rudy. He was Spanish and gorgeous. It seemed so real; the feelings were intoxicating. So genuine was it that I believed any day I would bump into him somewhere, at the grocery store with my mother or, better yet, at the movie theater with my best friend Joyce.

I spent quite a bit of fifth grade wondering about him, wishing he were real. There were no Hispanic children where I attended school, and I did not entertain a similar infatuation in waking life. Where had he come from? The details of the dream have long since faded; I only know that it left me with an intense longing for someone whom I had never met. Why I dreamt of him remains a mystery to me.

This memory serves to remind me of how very potent the dreaming process can be. It sometimes awakens and stirs desires we aren't yet aware we possess. If I had been keeping a dream journal at that young age, writing down the details of these nightly excursions, I would no doubt have clues to help me decipher the meaning of my prepubescent love dream. Was it a past-life memory? Or was it merely a half-forgotten remnant of a television drama I had recently seen, now re-created with myself as the heroine? I don't know. I only know it gave me goose bumps and several weeks worth of little girl fantasy. It wasn't until I began keeping a daily log of my dreams that I learned to unravel the intricate patterns held in these amazing storylines.

Over a period of years, I have begun to develop an instinct for whether or not a dream really needs to be written down and worked with in depth or simply acknowledged on the spot. Sometimes the meaning is quickly apparent, and I choose not to delve any more deeply than that. Other times I race to my notepad or tape recorder to preserve as much detail as possible.

Another aspect of dream work that became clear only after working with these nightly visitors for a while is that a dream is more than just a collection of symbols to be "figured out." Other elements such as the overall emotional tone, the intense or lukewarm feelings evoked, are often more revealing than simply determining what the snake dangling from the tree means. Bottom line: I learned to keep the symbology and other peripheral elements within the context of the entire dream experience. Excellent manuals that outlined the basics of dream interpretation, among them Mark Thurston's *Dreams: Tonight's Answers for Tomorrow's Questions,* became my tools. They provided common-sense methods for breaking the code of dreams on an ongoing basis. As with learning any skill, such as mathematics or grammar, the longer I work at it the more adept I become.

A series of dreams I had several years ago illustrated the metaphysical birthing pains that I was having as I worked at implementing spiritual principles into my daily life. As it is with many of us, fear seems to be one of my major issues, as was evidenced by these terrifying nightmares. The dreams began with various forms of natural disaster. Sometimes it was a tornado, other times an earthquake or fire. The fact that the method of destruction was ever changing led me to believe that these were not precognitive warnings; rather, they were indicative of an internal struggle of my own. In the dreams I would experience extreme panic and try to calm myself by reciting the well-known verse from the Twenty-third Psalm, "The Lord is my shepherd, I shall not want."

I would watch, trembling, as brutal winds tore the roofs from buildings, and cars were tossed into the air as though they weighed less than Ping-Pong® balls. The terror was immobilizing, but I chanted the psalm over and over in hopes of abating it. Each dream would find me repeating the words, with my inner resolve still weak. I said them as one facing sudden death might, with dread coursing through my veins, heart pounding, and a feeling of faint in my head. Gradually, though, the prayer became more than just a frantic plea.

One night as the dream invaded my consciousness once more, I found myself entering a Jeep® with my mom and brother, the three of us trying to escape an explosion that sent flames bursting through our neighborhood. I was frantically repeating the first line of the psalm, begging for mercy and help. I was seated in the back seat of the Jeep®, when suddenly I began to stand. A determined belief in the words grew, and I found myself shouting them with the full knowledge that it was so: "THE LORD IS MY SHEPHERD, I SHALL NOT WANT!!" There was power contained in that proclamation, and I was electrified by it.

Were my dreams mirroring to me the progress that I was making in applying faith in regard to my fears of "catastrophe" or whatever catastrophic circumstances and emotions that I was having to face in all their fury? Perhaps. I know that in my waking life my attitudes were under construction, or reconstruction rather. While I had by no means conquered fear in every area of my life, I was beginning to build a lasting and strong foundation for the knowledge that "all is well," as my *God Calling* book insists. In my dream state my progress in accepting faith was gauged by the strength of my conviction as I repeated the psalm.

In his book, *The Kingdom Within: The Inner Meaning of Jesus' Sayings,* John A. Sanford has this to say: "Our dreams are often filled with the image of the storm. We may be on a stormy ocean, or driving into a black cloud, or shaken by an approaching earthquake, or exposed to a driving wind and rain. In this time of storm faith is essential. But this is not an intellectual faith that consists in giving assent to creedal doctrines; it is an inner attitude, a committing ourselves to the inner way regardless of what comes, a determination to know the One who is at the center of the conflict."

It helped me to know that I was moving from sheer panic to a calm confidence, because fear of outward circumstances had long made me shudder and interfered with my ability to trust.

In the readings of Edgar Cayce I discovered the interesting theory that everything that happens in the physical takes place first in the spiritual realm. That can be a difficult concept to wrestle with, due to our three-dimensional perspective here on earth. However, it does provide some insight into just how precognition works. If an event is likely to happen, it will be given a "rehearsal," if you will, on the other side. While this doesn't mean that it is destined to be, since we can exercise our free will at any time to change the path we're on, it does supply us with an opportunity on occasion to envision things before they actually occur in our physical world. Such was the case when I entered sleep one night, only to be able to see beyond what my five senses usually allow.

It was soon after I had moved home to Illinois from the East Coast after spending a year living near Tom, getting to know him better and falling more in love. We were in for a long separation while he took on the demands of an internship in Baltimore. I needed something fun to take my mind off of missing him, and I looked toward school.

I was ready to explore areas I had not ventured into before. Instead of taking more science and math courses, as I had just finished a round of, I chose to take a semester to play. I scanned the list of classes offered by the community college and decided that theater production was just the tonic I needed to release the tensions of the past several months spent dealing with a tough college curriculum plus the emotional turmoil of separating from Tom. The course description wasn't clear about the content, and I wasn't sure if it entailed studying the history of theater or assisting in the production of an actual play. I would find out soon enough, but in the meantime I had the following dream:

> Dressed as a fairy-tale princess, I am at the front of a classroom reading from a book of such stories to the grade-school children at their desks.

With the dream neatly tucked away in my memory bank, I drove to the college for sign-ups a few days later. I sat with the instructor, who was happy to see me since enrollment was sparse. He explained that the class would participate in all aspects of producing a play: set design, costumes, props, and acting. From start to finish, the entire process was ours—with his help, of course. He then asked me to come to try-outs that evening. I was hesitant because I hadn't acted since playing Priscilla, one of the young female pilgrims who landed at Plymouth Rock, in my third-grade Thanksgiving play. He was adamant and persuaded me to try, explaining that there were not going to be enough students to fill all the roles, and already many of the parts were being read for by adults from the community theater group. I agreed to come, getting excited at the prospect of acting.

That night we gathered in a large classroom to take turns reading, as the instructor made notes and determined who would act in his autumn production. I stumbled through the lines, being extremely nervous and unsure of why I was doing this. It shocked me, therefore, when I learned two nights later the results of the tryouts: I earned the leading role in the play! Its title: *Beauty and the Beast.* Yes, I was about to begin preparation for my part as a fairy-tale princess. As the real-life drama unfolded, however, I would find myself facing a beast of my own: the ugly monster known as Rejection, a stepson of Fear.

All of the parts were filled. My instructor took the role of the Beast; his teen-age son was appointed the smaller one of the Prince who emerges at the end. My two sisters were played by wonderful actresses active in theater who brought humor and excitement to their roles. The narrator was a high-school student with a career in acting as her goal; Beauty's father and the merchant both veterans of community theater. We began rehearsals every Tuesday and Thursday night, and I recited my lines into a tape recorder to play before falling asleep.

The play was written entirely in rhyme, with such lines as, "If I can't pound logic into your head, then I'll impress the other end instead." It was done with professional finesse, which prevented the sing-song nature of the verse from becoming annoying. Together the cast and crew prepared props and scenery and worked at memorizing the cleverly constructed lines. My dress for the crowning scene in which I became a true princess bedecked in glory was sewn by a crew member's mother. It was breath-taking in mauve tones of thin silk and lace with a tall pointed hat that trailed a long silky pink scarf. I would be wearing a waist-length, strawberry blonde wig and thick false eyelashes to complete my transformation.

Finally, the big night arrived. Our first show was on a Friday evening, and I felt panic-stricken, yet thrilled. Once the play was under way I relaxed a bit and enjoyed the tense excitement that permeated the stage atmosphere. There were few bloopers, and the show seemed to go off without a hitch.

My enjoyment was short-lived. Saturday morning I awoke, happy, and ready to do two more shows. I knew that there was to be a review in our local paper, and I rushed out to the kitchen to read it. My mom simply handed me the paper without comment. I began to read what was a positive critique of our play, until I reached the end. Suddenly, my stomach collapsed to my toes. The writer seemed to enjoy the show and all the performances except one: Carolyn Kresse as Beauty. "While more than attractive enough for the part, she didn't act particularly moved during her climactic reunion with the Prince." There it was, in black and white. All I could do was return to my bedroom with stunned, wounded pride, and call Tom in Baltimore for reassurances and encouragement, which he gave as only he can.

I was crushed, and I had two more shows to do that very day. I had to be at the theatre in a few hours, so I pulled myself together and arrived in the dressing room before anyone else did to avoid walking in alone with all eyes fixed on me. I was applying my heavy stage make-up when my two "sisters" came in. I'll never forget their kindness or the way they helped build me up so that I could make it out on stage again. They comforted me by emphasizing that the reporter hadn't trashed my entire performance, just the final scene. They agreed that it was hard to look thrilled when the Prince was wearing a wig that made him look just a wee bit silly. We laughed and really grew close that morning. Then the two of them gave me some tips to improve my acting skills, and my confidence was rebuilt enough to give it another shot.

I could feel myself trying harder to truly "act" the part of a passionate princess. The critic's words had been hard, but true. My final scene definitely needed the rush of adrenaline that usually accompanies a lover's reunion. My performance was no Katherine Hepburn, but the criticism did spur me on to better a rendition for having been challenged. Afterward, some little girls came and asked for my autograph. At the cast party, the daughter of one of the prop women and her little friend drew a picture of me that said "To Beauty. We liked you in the play." The only review that really mattered was given to me in loving quietness from the people whom this was all for anyway, the children.

I thought of my dream. Yes, I had dressed as a princess and spoken fairy-tale lines to little ones, had helped weave a tale about sacrificial love in one of the more positive fairy tales available. In the process I was also reminded that no one is immune to the biting sting of censure and that it is necessary to sometimes do the hard thing, the thing we most fear—and do it with the help of our friends.

It is comforting to me to know that our lives are not just happenstance and that we have an internal resource that sometimes previews and prepares us for events to come. Dreams are part of this reservoir of power that comes from within. They can also serve to guide us out of confusion at key moments in our lives. I experienced this sort of guidance when I was walking through a very doubtful period of searching and questioning of my own beliefs.

It is easy for me to imagine people being enticed into religions that are very restrictive and controlling. It's not that they are necessarily weak minded or less enlightened. It is because, at least in my experience, the flooding with "facts," whether in the form of biblical quotations or others, is massive and powerful. I was working with another nurse from my hometown when I encountered this type of pull, and it was my confidence in the validity of dreams that helped me through it.

Belinda and I have a lot in common. We share the same birthdate and were born only hours apart. We both chose nursing as a profession, and we are both compelled to seek the spiritual meaning of life. The main difference in that latter common thread is that she belongs to a strict religious denomination that separates itself from other Christian sects and demands observance of Jewish laws, such as the Saturday Sabbath and the traditional feast days of Moses' time. Still, I was drawn to talk to her about her beliefs. I didn't have the courage to delve into an explanation of my own religious leanings, because I knew that her church feels that anyone not within its group is of the devil. I did not want to explore him at all!

Because of my curiosity, Belinda felt it her "duty" to try to convince me of the correctness of her position. She knew her Bible thoroughly and was well versed in her church's interpretation of it. We were working forty miles from our hometown, she driving the distance each morning after we finished the night shift, me living nearby in an apartment. One night it snowed very heavily while we were at work, and she wasn't able to make the drive home. I invited her to sleep at my place and return to work that night with me. She agreed.

Following eggs, toast, and chamomile herbal tea, I took out my Bible that I had been underlining and researching in response to our debates. The first problem with my position, as Belinda saw it, was that I was not using a "correct" biblical version. I was using the *Living Bible,* a paraphrased account which is easy to read. Her argument was that much of the original intent of the writers was altered and inaccurate. This was not going to be as easy as I thought. She was steeped in the teachings of her church, and I was not armed with the proper evidence to persuade her otherwise. More important, my emerging crisis revolved around the fact that I was being more and more convinced that she could be correct. My head was spinning from the deluge of Bible verses that she was tossing my way. I couldn't keep up. I began to feel sick to my stomach and suggested that we sleep for awhile. So, we each crawled into bed, exhausted, as the snow continued to swirl outside.

As I sank into the comfort and warmth of my bed, I prayed for help with discernment. Was it truth that Belinda spoke? If it was, I was definitely on the wrong path. It was with these thoughts of confusion that I entered into a fascinating dream.

I dreamt that I was in Virginia Beach at the A.R.E. Only, it wasn't the present day I was in—I had journeyed back in time. Edgar and Gertrude Cayce were still alive, and I was meeting them for a seaside lunch. We talked, and the two of them offered me guidance and suggestions. At the end of our visit I had a sense of relief and great happiness. Upon awakening, I could not remember the specifics of our conversation.

I awoke that afternoon truly refreshed. The feeling of nausea left, and it was no longer important to me to argue with Belinda and try to convince her of my "rightness." I still felt an interest in her faith; it carried an energy that moved me somehow, but I knew that on certain points we might never agree. I think she had begun to feel that way as well, and while not entirely cured of the tendency to try to persuade the other to see her error in thinking, most of the time we withstood that temptation.

I also began to realize that what I was labeling as a "restrictive" religion was undoubtedly what her soul had chosen and was really an admirable undertaking. After all, being true to her beliefs and following her own personal God were a true test of faith since it usually put her at odds with the rest of the world, including her own family. I don't know what Edgar and Gertrude had to say at our luncheon that day, but whatever it was I thank them for sharing a bit of their wisdom with me. I'm still trying to really learn and remember it for myself.

These last two dream experiences, and the real-life incidents which accompanied them, were very straightforward and simple. The first merely gave me a short preview of what was to come, an opportunity for me to communicate with children through the vehicle of a fairy tale. The second came as a response to a plea for help and was an obvious answer to my questioning turmoil about spiritual choices. These are not the most common of my dreams, however. Some are much more difficult to interpret. That is where the study group can be of great help in digging for meaning amidst a puzzling jumble of images and symbols. The first study group that I was a part of had members with many years of experience in working with dreams. It was then that I began the practice of writing my dreams down in order to work with them. Later, I bought a voice-activated tape recorder that I kept by my bedside. I found that if I captured the details on tape before completely awakening, I remembered much more. I learned in working with a group that sometimes the dreamer herself is blind to the obvious when it comes to difficult issues. The insight of a group member can shed the necessary light that brings the realization, "Exactly! Why didn't I think of that?" Such was the case for me when I came to the group one evening, dream book under my arm.

I was a twenty year old, still in nurse's training, and many times on the weekends we would all get together to party and have a good time. I had this revealing dream:

> I am at a party at someone's house whom I am unfamiliar with. The man who lives there hands me a drink which I know has been laced with poison. I realize I must escape.

I had tossed that dream around in my waking consciousness, unable to draw the meaning from it. Was someone going to actually try to kill me? Should I stay away from people I didn't know? Was the dream symbolic of being poisoned by the ideas of someone else? I honestly was not sure. It was Pam, our leader, who brought clarity to the matter.

In her wonderful, matter-of-fact way, she chimed in in the midst of another member's crafting of a rather complicated interpretation, "It sounds to me as if she's being poisoned by alcohol. Does that sound reasonable to you, Carolyn?" Ahhh . . . indeed it did. I knew that I needed to curtail my weekend fun and eliminate the "poisons" that my system was receiving, and my dream was simply reinforcing that conviction. Actually, this dream was pretty straightforward after all.

The group proved helpful on many other occasions when the symbology and story line became convoluted, as they often do in dreams. There is a synergy brought to the process when two or more combine their efforts and intuitions to help the dreamer sift through the list of possibilities.

Having chosen Jesus as my personal guide and master, it is not surprising that some of my dreams include visions of Him. This one was disturbing to me:

> I am among those who have come to see Him crucified at Golgotha. As I stand watching, I am gripped by an emotion that tears at my heart. (Imagine the pain of witnessing someone gentle and kind, someone you love beyond words, suffering the pain of being nailed to a wooden tree! "Unbearable" seems a vastly inadequate word for describing this feeling.) I scream, "That's enough. I cannot watch any longer!" Instantly the scene changes, and I am with someone I know as my grandpa (although in waking life I have never met him before). It's clear to me that he is on the other side, and I ask him how I am doing in regard to spiritual growth. He encourages me with positive affirmation of my progress. I then ask what I need to do in order to do "better." He instructs me to avoid excessive alcohol intake. The dream ends.

Interestingly, the second part which tells me to avoid alcohol was given at around the same time period as the poisoned drink dream. I was definitely being guided. The envisioning of Jesus' dying was excruciating to witness, and a similar experience has not come my way since. Another dream that involved Him was this:

> I come upon a large outdoor gathering. People are arranged theater style listening to a man speak. I become aware that they think he is Jesus and that the second coming has arrived. I know that it is not He, and I try desperately to convince them so. No one listens, and in my anxiety I consider killing myself in order to escape the horror of the entire world following this false prophet.

It deeply bothers me when I witness people placing complete faith in human beings who claim to have all the answers. But why the thoughts of suicide? In my dream I felt consumed by sorrow and fear at being the only one to not believe in this man. Perhaps this was a shadow of what I often felt in waking life. I have reached a point now where I am comfortable with people who believe differently from me, but at that time I wanted to share what I was learning with everyone and have them concur. Often I felt like an outsider when there were very few who actually did. I was around twenty at the time of that dream and over a decade has passed since then. It's just not as important to me now to convince any one of the "enlightenment" I have found, because I realize that I, too, see through a glass darkly, just as everyone else, no matter how spiritually evolved we think we are. We're here to learn, and I keep coming back to the fact that "Truth is many sided," as the *God Calling* book suggests. My side, while inspiring to me, is not the entire animal.

There is also the consideration, when reviewing this dream, that I have been influenced by stories of false prophets arising in the last days. While the preceding interpretation may be partially correct, there is also the possibility that a literal one is in order. I am not so arrogant as to believe that I would be the "only one" to actually see the lie for what it is, but maybe my dream was an exaggeration of events that will take place and a warning to me not to take the cowardly way out.

While it seems that dreaming is serious business, as indeed it is, there is also a playful, mischievous aspect as well. Sometimes it's necessary to laugh at ourselves, and I am one who needs constant reminders of this. The dream can be entertaining as well as instructive or even indulge us in pure fantasy from time to time.

As in the early childhood dream of Rudy, I still sometimes experience romantic crushes while dreaming, and it can be very amusing. I am a faithful fan of the television comedy, *Seinfeld*. I tape the shows so that I can watch them again, and I laugh even harder the second time around. One character I particularly like is George, "the bald guy." I would frequently mention to my friends how much I enjoy the show and remark that I "love George!" So I shouldn't have been surprised when he showed up in a dream one night as my boyfriend, and our laughter woke me. Dreams not only help us in a very serious way, they can also provide some comic relief on occasion! When I mentioned my dream to a friend, she remarked that it's not surprising, because the characters are a lot like my husband, who grew up in New York and has a very similar witty style. At any rate, I don't have to wait until Thursday night to enjoy the show, and if ever there is an extended power outage and I can't tune in, perhaps my subconscious will provide some diversion.

It's a wonderful gift, the ability to dream, and one we all share. I intend to continue to follow the Talmud's advice and keep viewing my dreams as letters, messages from within to be read, explored, and enjoyed.

# 7

# *Searching for God*

> "But if we walk in the light, as he is in the light, we have fellowship one with another..."
> —I John 1:7

THE search to find meaning and implement a growing body of spiritual knowledge into everyday practice, while among others who are also exploring, I have found nowhere as completely satisfied as in the Search for God study groups that I am fortunate to have been a part of. It is a unique place to lay a foundation for the spiritual life with others of like mind.

It is also a testing ground for discovering the weakest parts of ourselves, giving us the chance to confront and learn from them. Quiet agreement with noble principles made in the comfort of solitude is only part of the process of growth. The true test comes when opposition rears its head to demand response. How we respond is very telling.

In the summer of 1987 the opportunity to participate in the adventure of aspiring to the way of living that the study group offers was once more mine. I helped initiate the formation of the group while "stationed" again in Decatur. This would be my third since my special initiation during nursing school. The other groups were quiet continuations of what the first began for me. With Tom in Baltimore, my time was all mine, waiting to be filled with new friends who shared my enthusiasm for taking an avenue not often traveled.

The introductory night was held at my parents' home. Only a fraction of what would become the core group attended. It was shy and subdued, not any indication of what was to come. We decided to hold the meetings on a regular basis at the home of Adam, a young man who attended the first meeting. An unusual trend that developed was that most members were within a ten-year age span of one another. The exception was an older retired couple and my friends from the first study group, who joined us later on. My experience had always found me as the youngest, with most members many years my senior. Now the majority were between twenty-four and thirty-six. Age is not necessarily indicative of compatibility, but being young and single, I was happy to find peers who shared similar life experiences and attitudes.

Our first evening at Adam's house was incredible. He lived in a large, airy home that was warm and inviting. Candlelight and large soft pillows lined the cozy den where we gathered to begin our journey together. We were quite a mixed group. Debra, who had recently moved back to our hometown from Los Angeles, was exotic—with long black hair and huge eyes and a bubbly personality. She was unhappily doing secretarial work at the time, but her hidden passion was art: drawing, stained-glass work, and jewelry making. She also had a love of dance and was active in the Greek dancing that her church offered.

Two close friends and fellow singers were Deni and Sue. They each arrived in black leather biker jackets. Sue had a very short, spiked hair style accessorized by a skull necklace—obviously an independent, nonconforming spirit. Deni, reflective and intelligent, was a study in contradictions, with a raw wildness that enabled her to be a fiery lead singer on the weekends. Adam, our host, by day wore the conservative hat of executive and by night pursued writing and painting as his alter ego took over. His roommate, Billy, was a very social man, with a love of creating elaborate meals.

Rob and Meg, our retired over-sixty members, filled their days with quiet activity. Enrolled in art school, Rob now had the time to let his creative side blossom. Meg, a peaceful searcher who had had some experiences with the paranormal that left her questioning, came to the group ready to learn. June was an auburn-haired, thoughtful woman who had also attended my first study group several years earlier. She and Meg seemed to be the leaven in our unusual loaf, much more calm and easygoing than the rest of us. Then there was I, a nurse and frustrated poet-writer. The time had arrived for us to join our hearts and minds in anticipation of new discoveries.

There was such excitement in finding one another that it was difficult to contain ourselves. We were all so eager to talk that sometimes we would forget to limit our speaking time and would wander far afield. There was much to share, and the revelations seemed endless. We were peers on many levels, most of us with a flair for the dramatic and passionate in our opinions. When the meditation period was over and we shared our experiences that first night, what was usually a winding down time for most groups was just the beginning for us.

We moved to the dining room to feast on a mouth-water-ing array of food that Billy had prepared. There was a gorgeous, artistic display of fresh vegetables and dips and delicious cheeses and fondue. We indulged ourselves in food and fellowship.

Affiliation in a particular religious denomination is not a requirement in the ASFG groups. Jews, Buddhists, Christians, seekers of all faiths are welcome. The focus is on discovering God, not on limiting Him to a specific theology. Several of us in our new group shared a common history of Christianity—not the highly indoctrinated sort, but a friendship with Jesus that surpasses creeds.

I felt a kinship with Sue. She told me she had had a dream before meeting me, and in it I was dressed in white and carried a message for her and Deni. I have no special grasp on truth; I only share the piece of it that I've come to know, so I am sure that this dream's purpose was not to bolster my ego. I believe it was pointing her toward the study group and the messages they would receive as members united in purpose together. It's just that at that point I was the only link she had with our newly forming alliance since my name was on the invitation. She shared her love of Jesus and His influence on her life. Again, I felt a bond forming among us as we sat at the round wooden table.

With trust quickly developing, Adam told of an experience he was having that was disturbing to him and asked for our help. He said he had been feeling a strong negativity in his home and was unsure of its origins. I suggested a dream incubation—something I had participated in before with startlingly helpful results. Each of us would write down Adam's name and the specific request for guidance concerning this darkness. Every night we would pray over the slip of paper and place it near us, as we went to sleep with the intention of opening ourselves to the Holy Spirit's direction during the dream state. All agreed to this experiment, and the conversation lightened to carry us on past midnight. Then it was hugs all around and reluctant good-bys until next time.

Inside my car I became frightened. The dark streets seemed ominous, and I raced my big green 1978 Thunderbird (entrusted to me by Tom) over bumps and potholes to get home. I felt a bit like the cowardly lion of *The Wizard of Oz* after the wicked witch had lifted him unexpectedly into the air; like him I muttered to myself, half silly, half serious, "I do believe in ghosts! I do, I do, I do believe in ghosts!" Once home I quickly got under the sheets, prayed for the incubation, and drifted off into a fitful sleep. I awoke at 2:00 a.m. following a disturbing nightmare. I had been aware that I was dreaming and felt that I was receiving important messages for the incubation. However, a spirit of intense fear continued to wash over me. I couldn't speak in the dream, so I kept thinking the name Jesus over and over again in my mind. I was "almost angry," according to the dream journal I was keeping at the time. When I awoke, my throat felt parched. I went to the bathroom to get a drink because I didn't want to walk through the dark house, and when I looked in the mirror I almost screamed. My eyes were bloodshot, my skin blotchy. I didn't look like myself. The details of the dream had evaporated, and I returned to bed for an erratic sleep that carried me the rest of the night.

At the meeting the following week, I cautiously mentioned my scare. Part of our post-meeting conversation the week before had centered on bizarre supernatural experiences, and I felt that it had had an unpleasant effect on me. I requested a cease-fire concerning "ghost stories." Adam believed that my nightmare may have addressed his ongoing dilemma, so we prayed and followed Deni's suggestion of burning an Indian incense throughout the house to purify it of any unwelcome influences possibly harbored there. Whatever the source of my discomfort, it lifted and we carried on. What remained obvious to me, however, was that this group held a more intense emotional tone than any other I'd been a part of.

As time went on, we began to experience synchronicity among us. Similar challenges were coming our way, and often we were meeting one another in dreams. Week by week we met to open our books in eagerness for where our conversations concerning these valuable concepts would lead. Each lesson is designed to build upon the last. We began just as I had years earlier with the first group, by laying a foundation through studying the practice of meditation. There is nothing new about it; it is as old as time. Contemplative Christian orders have known its benefits for thousands of years. Eastern religions are perhaps most often cited as practitioners of entering the silence, but they only comprise a small group of devotees. It is not an occult practice as some would charge, for it is God who is being listened to.

While working with the chapter in the ASFG book that dealt with meditation, I had a dream which would later prove to be a clear indication that deep within I was aware that our group would face a dramatic opportunity for growth together. Our discipline for the week involved using specific aids at the beginning of meditation to enhance attunement (chantings, incense, exercise, music, etcetera). I had begun visualizing that I was giving Jesus my heart and brain in order to allow Him to sort out my "intellect and emotions." (I can sometimes become quite graphic—I suppose my years in nursing contribute to that tendency.) I awoke early that September morning to a dream full of luminous images. The following is an account of that dream:

> I arrived early at my study group to find the table set with bowls of golden broth and oyster crackers. I remarked to Billy how elegant it was. Everyone else arrived, and we sat down at the long table with Adam

and I at either end facing each other. Deni sat at my left, and I began discussing another dream with her, asking for her interpretation. Adam was not looking at me, and I became concerned that he was impatient for the meeting to start. I look at a clock that says 6:00, then five or ten minutes until seven (meeting time). I tell him that I have been praying for him, and he stands and says, "I was not listening to you, and now I will tell you what your dream meant." I feel that he can, but Billy interrupts and tells him not to. Billy is "high" on drugs, and he scares me. Adam then states that he wants to go get something to eat. An older woman (I'm not sure who she is) says she has to leave in twenty minutes. I'm afraid that we won't get to the lesson. I become aware that a party has been going on and the bowls of broth have been eaten from. (Three bears reference?) I'm glad I didn't taste it. We all leave, walking down the street to a restaurant. Outside, I buy Wheat Chex® mix; inside I would like to have the same thing with "toppings." Instead, I buy tacos. A girl from the group tells me that Billy prepared fillet of sole with tiny onions on top, soaked in wine. She warns me not to eat it and get drunk, and I tell her that cooking evaporates the alcohol. She disagrees. Back at the house Billy is saying, "I can't believe you're worried about the alcohol!" We are in the basement where a young man sets a match down on top of some things stacked against the wall, and the house catches on fire. We yell "FIRE!" as we run outside. I tell a strange girl that I know who caused it and I'm looking for him. She looks suspicious and I'm sorry I said anything. Then I become afraid that he'll find me.

I discussed the dream with the study group, as that was a valuable part of our work together. Like detectives, we would sift through the images and feelings in order to uncover their meaning. An incomplete and tentative interpretation that we worked out from these details was that our spiritual food was contaminated, first by other people, then by spirits (alcohol).

A trial by fire will perfect us through elimination of subconscious memories or fears (basement). Adam also felt that the dream was illustrating that his psychic abilities were being blocked by these subconscious elements. This was a rudimentary interpretation, focusing mostly on symbology. As I will explore later, that was only one layer of meaning contained in that dream.

By Christmas time, four months into the formation of the group, our numbers had grown. Pam and Samuel, the couple who had taught me so much in my first group experience, were among those who joined. They came with excitement and joy; the two of them love study group work and have been active in the A.R.E. for many years. Dave, both an owner of a construction company and a psychology student, added his thoughtful, quietly introspective presence. Along with these additions, there were a few others who occasionally dropped in to share the meeting with us.

We planned a big Christmas party to take place at Adam's house. When the night arrived, everyone from the group attended, as well as friends and spouses who were not members. The house was festive; a beautiful, sparkling tree in the living room, candlelight gracing the fireplace where logs were blazing, and the scent of Christmas dinner drifting throughout the house all created an enticing scene reminiscent of a Norman Rockwell painting. I had brought along a turkey that the patient I was caring for at the time had given each of us nurses as a holiday gift. Everyone else contributed his or her favorite festive dishes, and the result was a feast awaiting us. We were caught in the mood of good will, and everyone's spirits were high. I was very happy and grateful to be surrounded by my friends, my comrades in a spiritual quest!

We laughed, ate turkey and stuffing and all the other trimmings until we, too, were stuffed, then gathered in the living room to make music. Adam's deep baritone voice accompanied by his guitar led us in old-time carols, and Deni added her distinctive sound as we joined together in song. In the midst of our celebration, visitors appeared who would change the course of our group's future and truly unleash a fire beneath us. They entered in lively fashion, immediately capturing our attention. Lorraine and Bonnie were friendly and full of smiles as they joined in our holiday party, and everyone basked in the fellowship of the large group we had become. We socialized late into the night and reluctantly parted, as our holiday fiesta ended.

We were studying the chapter on "Faith," as the drama began to unfold. We were each applying every faculty of our minds and spirits in attempts to understand what was being presented in the ASFG handbook. Every chapter begins with an affirmation—a short quote from the readings designed to focus us on the subject being studied. This one began with: "Create in me a pure heart, O God! Open Thou mine heart to the faith Thou hast implanted in all that seek Thy face! Help Thou mine unbelief in my God, in my neighbor, in myself!" (262-13) We would soon need to apply these words in our relationships with one another. This chapter deals not only with faith placed in God, but in our brothers and sisters as well. It cautions: "Let us have more faith in our fellow human beings. We may not agree with them, but who knows whether they are not more in line with the divine plan than if they were following our lead?" (p. 44) How high a principle, easy to embrace in theory, but in reality it can be very difficult to live by.

As we prayed, debated, and made our way through our

weekly meetings, our Christmas party visitors returned once again. Lorraine and Bonnie arrived to join us as we read and discussed the nuts and bolts of exercising faith. In the midst of our usual lesson, somewhere during the discussion period, Lorraine came alive. She had been comfortably seated on the floor, mostly listening, when suddenly strange sounds began to arise from her. It sounded like gibberish, and I immediately recognized it as the phenomenon known as "speaking in tongues" written about in the Bible and practiced in some churches. She moved to Deni's side and gave her a "word of prophecy" concerning her grandfather whose health was failing. During the message, Sue began to cry and then interpret what was being said in the strange language: "Jesus is here. He says to reach out and touch His robe, there is no such thing as time." We were transfixed. No one moved or said a word, and many eyes were moist. There was a kinetic stillness in the room.

Lorraine carried a charisma about her. Tall, middle-aged, with silvery gray hair, intense eyes, and a large frame that combined to make her an imposing presence. For Adam she had become a mother figure, and he had prefaced her appearance that night by announcing that we had a "special guest" coming.

Bonnie was Lorraine's opposite in appearance. Painfully thin, with dark hair and loose jeans, Bonnie seemed fragile. When paired with Lorraine, however, her personality was strong and assured. For now she was quiet.

As the moment passed and the time for ending was near, I asked Adam what he had selected for the next week's discipline. Lorraine replied that God sometimes changes the program, and Bonnie echoed that sentiment by adding that books are not always necessary. We left it at that and moved to the dining room for our snack and talk session. We had had a moving and wonderful experience, and no one seemed disturbed by what had occurred. A few of our members had not attended that meeting and were in for a surprise at the next.

The following week when we met, a similar, but more forceful episode took place. With everyone present, Lorraine stood. She moved to the center of the room and began to speak again in tongues. Perhaps feeling spurred on by the last meeting's welcome acceptance of her, she proceeded with a sort of speech or sermon concerning our possibilities as a group to be a positive force in Decatur. She said that one day we would be able to walk into a room and have an effect on all those present. She compared us to spokes on a wheel, saying that Decatur was the hub of the nation, situated as it is in the center of the United States.

Lorraine gained speed as she spoke, whipping into a frenzy of emotion until she burst into tongues once more. Tears flowed down a few cheeks as she groaned and moved with conviction. Several faces, however, held a perplexed and uncomfortable look.

There was an icy quietness following the meeting, and some left without the usual "gab period" that our group enjoyed. I felt uneasy about the new turn our meetings had taken, but I wasn't quite sure what to make of it. I liked Lorraine and Bonnie, yet I was concerned that their disregard for books and formats might lead us completely away from the studies we had begun (echoes from my dream?). Still, I didn't want to be "stuck" in my ways, unable to move with the flow of spirit. Yet, by choosing an ASFG group we had selected the practice of purposeful spiritual discipline, and Lorraine seemed to pooh-pooh this important element of our structure. Disciplines ranged from the simply complex art of actively refraining from criticism to choosing a community project, such as distributing gifts to nursing home residents. These were gold. I went home that night confused, soon to discover that I was not alone in this feeling.

The week following the meeting found my phone lines busy, busy signaling calls from other members who wanted to discuss the incidents of the last two meetings. Some were mildly worried that we would lose our focus. Others were extremely unhappy with the new activities Lorraine had introduced. The remainder were perfectly satisfied with the recent turn of events. I remained unsure. My feelings seesawed between a "wait-and-see" attitude and a desire to set down some stricter guidelines for the meetings' format.

I thought of my first study group. I had been uncertain at first about the messages Julia relayed after meditation. The difference was that she had never attempted to draw all attention to herself or dismiss our desire for quiet study. Occasionally we drifted from the task at hand, but it was more the exception than the rule. With Lorraine, it seemed we were on the verge of drastic permutation. I began to feel that the answer lay in communicating our openness to all types of spiritual expression, while at the same time maintaining our weekly discipline.

We had met our first real obstacle together, and it was time to address it. We decided to have a meeting dedicated just to getting the issue out on the table and dealt with. Core members only attended; Lorraine and Bonnie did not. We gathered at Adam's girded by our own opinions and expectations. I had brought along a copy of the study group guidelines to help us weed through the matter with some guidance. So, with each of us having our own agenda set, we began to talk.

The hurt and anger were apparent almost instantly. Adam, being closely bonded to Lorraine, seemed particularly upset. Deni, our leader for the discussion, was trying to keep things focused, but tempers were flaring. As some of the older members spoke out about their belief that in an ASFG study group the format should be pretty closely adhered to, looks of scorn were cast their way. Someone

*Searching for God*

expressed the feeling that if the spirit of God wants to speak, we should not try to silence Him. To that came the reply that some did not feel that it was the spirit of God we were witnessing. Oh, if ever there was a doubt in my mind that this meeting was not going to end quietly, it quickly evaporated!

Clearly, battle lines were drawn, and emotions stretched tight—ready to fly at any moment. I was in shock as I sat and listened to some of my dearest friends unleashing poisonous verbal arrows at one another. That was my mistake, just watching. I did not try to step in and calm the situation, even though I was feeling strangely detached from it. It was like witnessing a crime taking place, only to stand by in horrified silence.

At one point Adam exclaimed that he was feeling a negative sensation coming from someone in the room, a potent case of "bad vibes." It wasn't until weeks later that I learned of at least four people who felt responsible for his distress. Voices raised, accusations flew, and there was no peace or cooperation to be found this night. The manual I brought lay unopened on the floor. I seemed to just allow myself to be hypnotized into inaction by something within that wanted to retreat. I was afraid. Afraid of the caliber of emotion that was heavy in that room. I chose to turn away rather than confront it.

Whenever there is a great potential for strength and unity, there is also a great risk of discord and destruction. We had veered from one path onto another very quickly. When the anger finally was spent, and everyone had quieted down, we parted. Some of us for the last time. Meg and Rob, the couple basically alone in their search until they found us, never returned. Bob felt injured by the incident, and despite phone calls and letters to him, he declined to continue as part of our group. I am sad as I think of that.

I remembered the dream. The spoiled food (also the spiritual implication of the fillet of sole—soul?—that has been contaminated by alcohol—spirits?), the concern for beginning the meeting on time, leaving to search for other "food," the fire that destroyed the house, and my fear of being "discovered" as knowing something about the fire's origins and being sorry I mentioned it to anyone, ready to hide in fear. Also, the dream within a dream that had Adam offering an interpretation without first listening to the details.

The symbols were clear to us at the time, but now I can look at them again, from the vantage point of time and experience. I know that many of us were distrustful of one another, myself included. We had set before us a banquet, and it was spoiled by fear—fear of others having already partaken of our cup, fear of unwelcome forces. Confronted by distrust and fear, we saw our place together as consumed by flame. And so it was. We continued to meet for several more months, but not in Adam's home any longer. The original passion had paled.

No one was to blame, and no one was blameless in our scenario. Each contributed in some way to the wonder of our beautiful beginnings, as well as to the ugliness of one night spent tearing unity apart. I had dwelled too closely in the dim light of my intellect and emotions, when I could have bathed our difficulty in a spotlight of prayer. There was great potential in our little group, and one day it will probably be said of us, as it was of many for whom Cayce did life readings, that "In this experience the entities both gained and lost."

We gained deep friendships that have survived the years, although we're scattered across the states. We gained a sense of lessons that seemed to be on fast forward, which is fortunate since we were together so briefly. The memories of those first few months are crystallized in my mind, and I know that others feel the same. Yet we were not unscathed by the current of emotions asserted that night. Some hurts were not healed, at least not among everyone.

In writing about these events my own perceptions were challenged. When I began reviewing the experience, I surprised myself by discovering that what I thought I'd learned was only a slice of the pie. I was certain that the major issue was how to keep a group on track and deal with distractions, and I intended to neatly tie this chapter together with suggestions for doing just that. My belief that things do not happen by chance forced me to go a level deeper.

The *Group Dynamics* manual (now out of print) says that: "Communication requires knowing something about what is on the mind of the communicant. Listening to his or her side may be far more important than anything we say and far more instructive. Unless we listen, we tend to talk not to people but to stereotypes, and we are getting only an illusion of communication." (p. 37)

I am now convinced that our major problem was not Lorraine or even the disruption she symbolized. Instead, it was our attitudes that were questionable. She simply presented us with the opportunity to practice what we were learning, the chance to listen to one another without prejudice and with the certainty of our correct position left outside the door. For me, it was also the occasion to intervene rather than shrink from a moment speeding out of control. These new layers of meaning gave me cause to remember that our deepest lessons are often not without struggle and are never as simple as they would seem at first glance.

"Create in me a pure heart, O God! Open Thou mine heart to the faith Thou hast implanted in all that seek Thy face! Help Thou mine unbelief in my God, in my neighbor, in myself!" (262-13) The wisdom of those words hauntingly reminds me of the need to begin each day to really live them.

# 8

# For Love of a Friend

> "Greater love hath no man than this, that a man lay down his life for his friends."  —John 15:13

SOMETIMES I've heard Christianity spoken about as if it is the amoeba of spiritual evolution, a preschool warm-up in the halls of learning. Unfortunately, as a result of myriad religious wars both on battlefield and home front that we have waged in the name of Christ, those labels may at times be well earned. The phenomenal power contained in the Christian faith is not what makes the front page, and half-truths and misunderstandings result. The good news is that the steps of the Master lead to wisdom that transcends the religion formed around Him—and provide a way for achieving the high ideals chosen in places such as the

Search for God groups or church.

I once found following Jesus an attraction as well as a repulsion when I considered some of the hypocrisies that I thought were part of the package. Over time, I began to realize that an intimate relationship with this Man was not only possible, but that the elements of distaste that some traditional teachings left me with did not have to deter me from following Him at all. In fact, learning to exist within a world of paradox and contradiction is my true challenge. It is necessary to retreat from it at regular intervals, but just as necessary to return.

As a child, I learned the basics of the Christian faith very early. My parents were not religious in the strict sense, which was fortunate considering my nature. I was spared what might have been the backfiring results of being forced to attend church each Sunday and instead was allowed some freedom to choose. Because of this, I cherished every Sunday spent hearing tales of walking on water and of a touch that could restore sight to blind eyes. Time spent at Little Galilee Christian Assembly, singing "Cum ba Ya (Come by Here), My Lord" around a campfire and listening to lakeside vespers messages, brought inspiration to break up the lazy summer days.

I was immensely intrigued by this miracle-working Man who once walked the streets of Palestine. At ten I was baptized in the Christian Church, completely in awe as I was immersed just as Jesus was, but in a baptismal font rather than in the Jordan River. In quiet, private moments I had no doubt that I believed in Him, but felt perplexed about certain aspects of the faith that the church was presenting. I sensed that there was more to the story than we had available to us. The concept of "accept Jesus or be lost forever in a sea of fire" was a big turn-off to me. It felt much too simplistic and cruel. It also inspired fear, which is something that I definitely did not need more of and which I found completely out of character for a God of love!

I faced a dilemma in battling my apprehension at the notion of hellfire and brimstone, especially when it came to my family. One Saturday night my parents and I were at my Aunt Barbara's home having our usual marathon "kitchen table" session of talk and laughter. It scared me that they were having cocktails. My church was against alcohol in any amount, thus I felt deeply disturbed and frightened at the prospect of my mom and dad and other relatives being "lost" to Satan's hold because of their beer-filled glasses. I decided to intervene on behalf of their souls.

With the help of my younger cousin, Cathy, I devised a plan. Then, with Bible in hand we marched onward to the kitchen to deliver a sermon on the dangers of drink! Cathy stood beside me in three-year-old innocence, while I, a mature ten, pleaded with them for their salvation's sake. I can clearly see us, standing serious and erect as I spoke. My dad reassured us by pointing out that Jesus' first miracle was changing water into wine at the wedding feast, and reluctantly we retreated from our pulpit. Knowing that there were rules that we were instructed to keep in order to make it to heaven weighed heavily on my heart, and I can imagine the hefty dose of parental guilt that my preaching must have stirred!

It was incidents such as these that created doubt in my mind. Not doubt of the love of Jesus, for that was and is unshakable, but uncertainty that His true message was being communicated by the modern-day church. There was a hunger within me for more. I was filled with inspiration each time our minister delivered a sermon about the loving nature of God and the friendship offered by Jesus. I wouldn't trade that early training for the world. But I was unsure about the unyielding emphasis on spiritual dos and don'ts that seemed harsh to me. In all fairness, I realize now that rules are sometimes necessary, otherwise there are those—

myself included—who have difficulty in exercising restraint. The many alcohol-related deaths and diseases are testimony to that fact.

Unfortunately, it doesn't leave room for human choice and discernment that are so crucial to growth. However well meaning a particular church's pet rules are, they can be a stumbling block, especially when the spiritual life becomes an all-or-nothing endeavor. I was uncertain and had simply to begin to piece the rest of the story together as the tools became available. Spellbound, I read as the Edgar Cayce readings told the story that helped me begin to complete the rest of the puzzle.

The infinite nature of the soul, beginning and ending not with our birth and inevitable death, but extending backward as well as forward: reincarnation. This philosophy is something I believe, not believe *in*, but simply believe to be true. I say that because it is not a religion, merely something that adds to my chosen belief in Christianity. It is a missing element that when discovered helped me to make some sense of the grand scheme of things. I do not presume to say that I found The Truth in this notion of continuing lifetimes, for truth cannot be encompassed by any single system of thought. I uncovered a part of the truth that for me was essential to my understanding.

One wonderful thing that embracing reincarnation did was allow me to release the fear of death and eternal separation from God. I know now that seeing our lives as existing on a continuum frees me to concentrate on the real nitty gritty issues, including discovering Christ more and more in my life and putting that experience of love into expression. A closer study of the Scriptures in the light of this belief revealed to me that Jesus taught the basic principles of this philosophy.

The Master said that "with what measure ye mete, it shall be measured to you again." (Matthew 7:2) This is the law of karma or meeting oneself, as Cayce put it, that Jesus was talking about. We build for ourselves consequences that must be met, either in karma or through His grace. Initially, when my dad began mentioning the theory of reincarnation, I rebelled. I felt that it was dangerous to delve into the whole area, that it was steeped in occultism and somehow evil. By reading and exploring what Edgar Cayce actually said about the subject and finding Bible references pointing to its validity, I grew into acceptance.

Two books that later on appealed to my mind with their strong Christian orientation were Lynn Sparrow's *Edgar Cayce and the Born Again Christian* and *Reincarnation: Claiming Your Past, Creating Your Future.* These filled in the spaces that helped bring together a more complete grasp of the theory that we are born again and again in the earth, trying to grow to heaven with the help of the Lord.

The passages that leaped from the pages as I studied the Scriptures for myself contained pointed references to reincarnation. I found Jesus being questioned by His followers about the prophecy that states that Elias [Elijah] must come again. The clear answer that Jesus gave was that Elias had come and wasn't recognized, followed by the statement that the disciples understood that He was speaking of John the Baptist. (Matthew 17:13) And in Matthew, Chapter 11:

> 11) Verily I say unto you, Among them that are born of women there hath not risen a greater than John the Baptist; notwithstanding he that is least in the kingdom of heaven is greater than he ...
>
> 13) For all the prophets and the law prophesied until John.
>
> 14) And if ye will receive it, this is Elias, which was for to come.

These verses were like newly discovered gold to me, with

their incontrovertible support of reincarnation. Release from fear was only the first of the gifts this new belief would give me. Over time, understandings have woven together to produce a totally new outlook on life, with emphasis on personal responsibility (reaping and sowing) rather than the punishment of God, as well as forgiveness and the all-important gift of grace. Just when I think the picture is almost complete, new revelations come to show me just how limited yesterday's view was.

Incorporating this belief into my own personal theology did not serve to make finding out who I may have been in previous lifetimes a burning issue for me. I have never received any specific psychic readings concerning it. Nor have I spent enormous energy trying to figure it out myself. Conversely, I'm not opposed to or fearful of knowing and have a strong sense of some of my earlier lifetimes.

For me it was more an experience of "Yes! This is part of the truth I need to help me make sense of things," and the subsequent learning centered on principles and spiritual laws. Specifics have never been that important to me, although I am curious. What is more important is to begin understanding and growing enough so that reincarnation will soon not be necessary. I no longer feel pressed to have others agree with me that reincarnation is a fact of life, although that tendency was there in the beginning. It is enough that I find help in its reality.

What surprises and concerns me more is when I am misunderstood because of my relationship with Jesus Christ. One late evening at a conference in Virginia Beach, I sat sipping wine with a friend. In a place such as the A.R.E., where people can regularly be heard having heart-to-heart talks about such things as spirit guides and out-of-body experiences, I feel it is not too much to ask that my personal guide be acknowledged. Consequently I was puzzled when my friend looked at me and expressed her resentment at hearing me speak of Jesus. She explained that her belief is that He is "no different than any other spiritual teacher, such as Buddha." I hadn't said that He was, but evidently her annoyance at the fact that I might believe it to be the case forced her to speak out.

This was sticky. I do believe that there is a difference. Challenged, I decided to declare it. I didn't want to alienate her by emphasizing our differences, but I was tired of walking on eggshells with people whom I was cautious not to offend. I had swung in the opposite direction in response to the door-to-door Bible-toting evangelist Christians, by trying to keep a low profile when talking about my faith. This time my early roots rose up to take hold of the situation by defending the cross.

"Their message might be the same, but I believe their mission was different," I tried to state in as unargumentative a tone as I could manage, though I could feel the blood rising to my cheeks. "Jesus died and then resurrected so that through Him we can all conquer physical and spiritual death. That means that karma no longer has to be met in the old 'eye for an eye' way. Our awareness is raised; what He did we can do, by linking His overcoming strength with ours!" This is my understanding, and I was tired of tiptoeing around it. His message of love is only part of the story, and if He had intended to leave it at that, death and resurrection would have been a sick joke. He showed us MORE! With my cards on the table, I hoped my words wouldn't cause an irreparable rift in our friendship.

I could see by the sparks in her eyes as they darkened that what I said was not acceptable to her, and I nervously took another sip of the Chablis as I tried to change the subject. It made me uncomfortable, but I am glad that I spoke out when confronted, since in past situations I have simply put my own conviction aside in order to maintain "peace." I, too, had often felt offended by Christians who insisted that if you didn't subscribe to their brand of religion, you were in danger of damnation; but I didn't have to stand by while the baby went the way of the bath water.

Yet Jesus reminds me not to judge another's belief system, that there are many paths upward. It's a balancing act sometimes to discern when and when not to speak out. I try to respect everyone's right to find his or her own way, but at the same time I feel compelled to defend the bad name that the term "Christian" has sometimes created for itself. It is the mistakes of we who profess this faith that cause that word to conjure up feelings of disgust and disdain. I simply want people to realize that in its purest form it presents a spectacular opportunity for growth.

The *God Calling* text dated March 4 says: "Remember that truth is many sided. Have much tender Love and Patience for all who do not see as you do." Just as I am asking that others have such patience with me, in allowing me to bear the title Christian and all that that term may evoke without evaluating its worthiness, I need to accept their opinions and beliefs as well. A phrase that I learned in one of my study groups is to "agree to disagree." In other words, don't feel that it is necessary to convince others to adopt your own belief system in order to feel validated. We can accept one another without holding identical spiritual attitudes. I have to admit that I'm much more comfortable when my discussions with others don't lead to disagreements, but being comfortable is not what it's all about. The writer of the famous "Desiderata" counsels wisely to: "Speak your truth quietly and clearly."

We are not to pound our opinion into the ground by producing "proof" of our rightness. Not scream and yell until the other person has to hear us and take notice. Not avoid saying anything that others might not agree with. Rather, speak truth quietly and clearly (and remember that truth is many sided). It's as simple and as difficult as that. (I'm finding that most basic truths really can be quite difficult to practice when it comes to discarding old habits!)

I am continuing to learn that it is really the experiences with the Divine that bring us closer together, rather than a focus on theology and the intellect. A moment which captures that fearless feeling of *knowing* and spreads peace to another is just a glimpse into the mind of Christ. All dearly held beliefs aside, just tender appreciation for the possibilities contained in joining together. Ideas are truly marvelous, but they pale in comparison to this ideal.

Come with me as I try to recapture with words an encounter which is really beyond any human language's ability to reveal. Through my sharing, perhaps we will forget for a moment that we are different and just know that we are one.

I had begun having my daily meditation periods sitting in the screened-in porch overlooking the lake surrounding the rear of my apartment. The sun sparkles on the water, as ducks float lazily along. Trees line the perimeter of the lake, giving me the feeling of being tucked away in a rustic cabin somewhere. One particular day I sat watching the water and the trees moving with the breeze, as I prayed with a copy of my *A Search for God* handbook at my side.

"Lord, what do I need to learn most right now in my life?" The answer came as a thought that I knew was from Jesus, "Unconditional Love." This was heaven, and I savored the moment. "O.K.," I prayed, "how do I go about learning it?" The reply, "By living with me." I then asked the Lord to guide me to a passage in my ASFG book that would be helpful in enhancing my understanding. His adamant yet loving command was, "Put the book down! Be with Me."

I sat with the warmth from the sun encircling my toes, confessing my sins, the areas where I had fallen short of the mark. Asking for help and affirming my desire to live with Him. Gratitude began to well up from within me, along with a profound sense of joy. I gave thanks for the relationships in my life and the lovely place I was living in. I was at peace as Jesus said, "You have here before your eyes what some have to work with much effort to visualize." As I sat absorbing the moment, He led me to pick up my book and turn to page 126. It read:

> "Lo, I am with you alway, even to the end of the age." If humanity could get the vision of what it means to love as He loves, what peace would come on earth!
> 
> Do we want the best for another before our own wants and desires are satisfied? Can we see some good in all whom we meet? This is the Christ way of showing love. Where we are weak, He is ready to sympathize, comfort, and supply strength. In His name there is power. If we call on His name, if we abide in His teachings, we will radiate such a glow of righteousness (right thinking and acting) that those who sit in darkness will see great light.
> 
> Let us take hold on things of the spirit, for they alone are eternal. "The children of Light are called even now into service that His day may be hastened, lest many faint." Do we not remember our years and years of service for our families and for our friends, in which every act was so prompted by love that there was never a thought of being weary? When our best years have been spent for them and we are no longer needed or seemingly appreciated, does sadness fill our hearts? Let us not forget that such service is never lost, for with love it has been woven into the souls of those for whom we worked. It will shine forth again and again in the lives of many yet unborn. Love never dies; it is eternal.

The poetry of this paragraph deeply moved me, especially since it was shared between my Lord and me. In meditation I always longed for the still, small voice to be a bit more audible and yet was content with the silent peace it brought. I learned in my study group that while hearing distinct messages is wonderful, it is the inner transformation that occurs whether we hear anything or not that is essential. This always satisfied me. Now I had experienced a breakthrough! His presence was very tangible, not merely the ethereal knowing to which I was accustomed. Again, a spirit of gratitude welled from within.

Another aspect of this quote that intrigued me was the statement that "The children of Light are called even now into service that His day may be hastened, lest many faint." Who are the children of Light? Whether they are those on earth who have achieved or are seeking a measure of spiritual illumination, saintly souls who have reached oneness with God and have gone on, those of us who struggle on the spiritual path, or all of these, clearly we all have a mission in preparing the way for the Lord.

While hearing voices might be a frightening prospect to some, I am convinced that direct guidance is going to be crucial in the coming days. If the earth changes predicted by Edgar Cayce and others are literally going to come to pass, it is imperative that we have a link with divine mind that is clear and strong. There is some controversy within the spiritual community about whether these predictions are to be taken symbolically or as actual possibilities. (I say *possibilities* because Cayce affirmed that free will was the ultimate governing agent and that through prayer and the resulting raised awareness the upheavals could be lessened or eliminated.) In her appearances in Medjugorje and other areas, Mary, the mother of Jesus, also points to physical changes of our earth that are potentially forthcoming. One of the messages that I understand to be central to her purpose in communicating with us is that now is the time to turn our attention inward to the God we might know and through prayer prepare for the coming uncertainty and vast change.

With many of the recent harsh weather conditions, earthquakes, hurricanes, storms, and floods, I am becoming more and more sensitive to the knowledge that we can be rendered almost helpless by nature in the blink of an eye. It's frightening, and it serves to impress upon me that I must be diligent, now as never before, if I am to keep the connection strong between my conscious mind and the mind of Christ and survive such a calamity. Jesus said to fear not, but He also expressed concern for pregnant women and children who would be fleeing in the "last days." His encouragement was tempered with a warning; and I am counting on Him to keep me posted on the latest developments concerning this unstable, rotating planet we are on.

He said that He is coming again and that statement is repeated in the Cayce readings. Cayce said that Jesus would come again in the body He occupied while in Galilee. My understanding of the readings is that not everyone on earth will recognize Him, however, and that knowing Him before He comes is a prerequisite for this sight (another strong motivation for not neglecting times of prayer and meditation while the air is still). Another possible reason for not distinguishing Him from the crowd could be that many of the circulating portraits of Him are so pathetically illustrative of a weak, helpless man. This rendition of my Master is totally incongruent with what I know of Him.

Jeshua, as He was known in His native tongue, is a Jewish Man who walked many miles across the sun-drenched hills of Israel. For this reason, I can't imagine Him the puny, pale caricature of a human that I see hanging in some churches. His earthly father, Joseph, earned his living as a carpenter and in the Jewish tradition, no doubt, his Son shared in that work as well, earning the callused, working man's hands. Again, the Cayce readings provide a wonderful view of His life that the Bible is silent about. They tell of a man with a sense of humor, something I would expect of one so enlightened. That facet of Him might throw someone off who was expecting a frowning, depressed-looking, sad little man.

Writing about Him, I feel my heart pounding faster as I imagine His return! What a reunion it will be, to see and touch Him, to sit with Him as He shares stories and laughter with all of us. It's like being separated for years and years from a wise and loving older brother, with only a telephone's weak connection to link us, fleeting moments of recognized closeness. That is how I feel, for although prayer has brought Him as close as a breath, for me there is still the longing for physical experience of this One I love so much.

Perhaps it's because I am still muddling through in my limited body and haven't even come close to the summit that I place so much importance on this event. Still, if it was not justified, He would not be coming back as the human being He was when on earth in physicality two thousand years ago. I believe He will, and I am preparing for it as best I know how. I want to hear Him laugh, share meals and work time with Him and all whom I love. I want to be ready when He arrives! On the altar of the Christian Church I grew up in there was a wooden sign that read, "We'll work till Jesus comes," and I suppose that will be engraved in my memory forever.

In the meantime, this intimate friendship must be nourished continually for it to remain alive. Just as ignoring any earthly relationship can result in a weakening of the bond, the connection with Jesus can wither from lack of attention. He is knocking, but He doesn't burst in without invitation. Where does this door lead? My *A Search for God* book explains in the chapter entitled "The Open Door":

> As we, with the Christ Consciousness as the stan-

dard, manifest His love in our daily walks in and before others, so we open the door . . . Let us know that when we speak a kind word or lighten the care of a neighbor, we open the door that He may enter, and through Him is the way into the Father's Kingdom, and there is no other. (pp. 83-84)

This chapter goes on to emphasize the need for service and becoming a door to our fellow human beings. Strongly accented is the need to emulate the compassion of Christ for all others. *God Calling* on April 18 states it beautifully, "Love is God. Give them Love, and you give them God."

It isn't a set of rules or a lengthy indoctrination that this world needs, it is simply love. Jesus Christ is a way-shower, a light-bearer, and embodiment of that perfect love. Christianity provides a powerful method of scaling the heights by offering this man as a go-between, an advocate with the Father for all who seek. Why do we need an advocate? Certainly He never forced Himself on any, and it is not my intention to do so either, but His help is available to all who desire it. To make connecting with God a little bit easier for all of us.

I have devoured as many books as I can get my hands on, both traditional and nontraditional alike, concerning the life of Jesus and His mission in the world. One in particular that held my interest was *A Life of Jesus the Christ,* by Richard Henry Drummond. I am perhaps prejudiced toward it since it combines the Cayce readings' unique perspective with the biblical scholarship of our time. In it, the author makes this enlightening statement about the church of Jesus:

Indeed, one definition of the church is that He (Jesus) who "was set as the head of the Church is the church" (262-87; compare Matthew 16:13-20). The same reading goes on to specify that Jesus' role is central in the life of the church, that its "membership" consists of those who are in relationship with Him as the Head of the church, accepting Him as Mediator between God and oneself, between one's self and other selves... "the true church is within you, as the Master, as the Christ gave... 'I to *you* am the bridegroom—I to *you* am the church. The kingdom is within *you!*' " (452-7; compare Luke 17:20-21; Mark 2:19-20; John 3:29). (pp. 188-189)

This chapter continued by saying that while the Cayce readings didn't give special preference to any particular denomination, they recommend formal worship for its centering effect on the mind. I have attended many different houses of faith and manage to find something uniquely helpful in most. Once I was invited to a largely African-American Baptist Church that was having a revival. The powerful voices that expressed an emotion that came from down very deep were incredible.

I had a moving experience in a Jewish synagogue. The prayers, songs, and general ambience of the temple brought the surge of inspiration and feeling of connection that I cherish. Ultimately, it depends on where I find that I can be of help and where I receive renewal that determines what type of service I do or do not attend.

In the Cayce reading just quoted, Jesus is described as a Mediator not only between one's self and God, but between man and man as well. (I use "man" as Genesis did when the writer stated that "In the beginning God created man—male and female." To me this term includes both genders.) I think that this aspect of His work is often overlooked. I know it was many years before the realization of that promise fully dawned on me. If we are having difficulty with someone, Christ is there to interpret between us if we ask. That is why it is so essential to pray for that intervention before meeting with someone to discuss an important matter or to ask for help in situations where understanding is lacking. Our minds are generally more restricted than His, and He offers His unlimited assistance to us.

He promised that we could do more than He did while on earth because He went to the Father. He finished the race, met the goal, and now bridges the gap for us still struggling on earth. True disciples live scattered throughout the world, in every religious and nonreligious faith there is, and no doubt they fulfill His vow.

It's just hard to believe sometimes when there is so much counterfeiting done in the name of the Lord. It turns people off, turns them away. My friend in Virginia Beach stands justified in her anger if we consider the lies told in His name. But we must look beyond. We must look within. Jeshua waits there, ready to assist us in loving a love-starved generation.

# 9

# Village of Faith

"Let not your heart be troubled, neither let it be afraid." —John 14:27

SOON I would need my Master's powerful, healing love in my life as never before. My partner and I still had mountains to cross before we could fully enjoy the miracle of finding one another. Jesus alone held the ability to find me in my dark place.

Soft candlelight, stillness, and the awareness of God's eternal calm. It is a feeling that surpasses all others. Experiencing this sensation of well-being becomes all the more valuable with the realization that if not guarded and nurtured, it can be ripped away violently in the trenches of life by one overriding emotion: fear! My *God Calling* manual states that "Depression is the impression left by fear" and warns over and over again to fight fear, "fight it as a plague."

How appropriate an analogy. The plague often spreads via rat fleas scavenging for a replacement host once the original has died. This demon-rat is powerful when allowed a stronghold, and continually Jesus finds it necessary to reassure us to "Let not your heart be troubled: ye believe in God, believe also in me." (John 14:1) The value of this teaching became clear to me when I experienced my own shadow-filled valley and had to work like thunder in order not to drown in my fear.

Looking back at this difficulty in my life, I can acknowledge that it was a necessary period of change. Confronted with my own personal devil, there was nowhere to turn but within. Given a choice, however, I'd much rather learn my lessons in a more gentle manner, by not allowing myself to neglect my prayer and meditation practices. By staying so close to the center that nothing can harm me. I believe that if I had been more diligent in seeking God on a regular basis, I could probably have weathered the storm more confidently and with far less fear. The strength of my spirit was not at its highest level when my world began to crumble, and I had to reestablish my relationship with Jesus at the same time that I was dealing with heartbreak in another.

After the study group dwindled, I strayed from my spiritual disciplines. Likewise, Tom and I had also drifted apart. We had endured a year apart while he finished his internship, during which hectic schedules and financial difficulty had made our visits together few and far between. That year ended, though, and we could begin again, as he started a three-year residency in St. Louis, only a two-hour drive from my home. It seemed our time in Egypt had ended. I would soon realize that it had only just begun.

During our year apart, we had agreed that we could date other people if the occasion arose, and I had casually socialized with friends of the opposite sex, but held back from really dating. The heart seldom listens to reason in these matters, however, and I was stunned by the news that he had taken advantage of our agreement without my knowledge. Disbelief soon turned to panic, and I struggled for weeks afterward to develop a sense of calm. Instead, my anxiety level soared. My meals remained untouched; before long size-three pants hung loosely on my small frame, and I developed a horrible case of eczema on my hands. The skin peeled away like snakeskin and became rough and reddened, lined with cracked open areas. I was a mess, inside as well as out.

Once my sense of security had been disturbed in this important area of my life, the plague quickly spread to find entry in others. During an in-service for a new hospital position I accepted, I watched a film concerning AIDS that left me paralyzed with terror. The possibility that I might have contracted the deadly disease when I worked at my first nursing job a few years earlier grabbed me and held a knife to my throat. At that time strict blood precautions were not yet instituted, and I had suffered needle sticks twice (once with a patient's syringe who was suffering from hepatitis—luckily I had tested negative for that frightening illness). I also spent one bloody night in the recovery room as the postoperative patient vomited copious amounts due to internal hemorrhaging.

It is no accident that the illness I chose to fear was AIDS. Hepatitis is actually much more easily spread by accidental needle sticks such as occur in a hospital setting, but I didn't dwell on that fear for even a moment. Acquired Immune Deficiency Syndrome is not only a disease of the body, but a panic-driven social stigma as well. Our history in handling this new epidemic left trails of rejection, hatred, and ignorant persecution. With my self-regard at its lowest, it was fitting that I include such a paranoia in my bag of horrors.

Living for even such a short time with this black cloud above me made me much more sensitive to those faced with a positive HIV status. A local hospital was doing routine testing for any health-care employees who desired it, and with a trembling heart and hands I underwent the withdrawal from my vein that would either abate or escalate my terror. Three days of suffering in silence, imagining every possible unhappy ending followed. I have never experienced such intense fear before or since. Prayer was of a frantic type, and eating was out of the question. The most I could manage to force down was a few saltines with water. Finally, the wait was over. It was negative.

Even while breathing a sigh of relief at being free of all blood-borne disease, the dread in my mind continued. There was no stronghold, no point of certainty in my life any more. The ordeal was gradually weakening me and pulling away any false sense of power or security I might have been living with until then. Fear had definitely left a deep impression on my body and soul. Work was a dreadful experience, and the full-time classes that I was attending were hell. Daily I had to force myself to get up in the morning and face the day. Tears would flow unexpectedly; one day it was during my poetry class while the instructor read love sonnets. Another time in the midst of algebra the instructor's shirt and tie reminded me of similar ones that Tom wore.

I felt that I was miserably failing this test of faith. At home I became a hermit, locked away, not really wanting to see or talk to anyone. The pain was palpable to everyone around me. The afternoon my dad gingerly asked me what was wrong and if he could help touched my heart. I don't remember many times when he ventured into my personal realm, and I knew it was a true act of love. No one could really get to the place inside that was hurting, however, no one but Jesus.

I began to spend much time in the quiet chapel at the hospital where I was working. The stillness that permeated the tiny room helped me to quiet my troubled heart and mind, and I felt uplifted by the soothing atmosphere of prayer. Until now I had been drifting along my spiritual path with no real stones in the way to block my progress. Nothing shook me to the bones as this had. I was learning to truly trust in the Lord with all my heart, mind, and soul. He was becoming my best Friend, my only Companion as I battled my personal demons of fear and self-doubt. Maybe this was what the saints were talking about when they gave thanks for persecutions, for by my own self-persecution during this hard time I was developing a much deeper relationship with the incredible Man I had chosen as my Guide in life. For this I give thanks.

One intimately tender gift that Jesus gave during this period was the knowledge that by my experiencing the pain of rejection I was making a closer link with Him and that He understood what I was feeling and would share it with me. He knew the pain of isolation and misunderstanding when His friends abandoned Him in His final hours. Peter's denial was more wrenching than the stab wound in His side. On an infinitely smaller scale, I felt this "aloneness" and the pain of feeling cut off from someone who had once known me so completely. I hung on to this revelation during times when my heart felt heaviest.

I can also see now from my comfortable vantage point that Tom and I each needed this shake-up in our relationship in order that we might move forward. I had become much too lackadaisical in my attitude toward him, and he had also lost some of the original devotion that he once had for me. It is often not until we almost lose something that we begin to truly appreciate it in all its unique wonder. The poets are right about that one! Leafing through my dream journals, there was evidence that I could see this coming long before I was consciously aware of the facts.

Quite some time before our period of separation, I had a very revealing dream. In it, Tom and I are standing on a platform that extends from a house. Suddenly it begins to break, and we fall through space before landing at the North Pole. Next, we are falling again, holding hands and praying until we land on the moon! At the time of the dream I puzzled about possible meanings, but now I could see that our foundation had certainly become insecure, and we were spending time "on ice" so to speak. Could the moon be representative of a honeymoon? Only time would tell. Interestingly, I had also recorded a dream that I had during our time apart in which I saw him kissing the cheek of a dark-haired girl who looked a little bit like me... precognition was in full swing that night.

Oh, how we can see our mistakes so clearly through the crystal lenses that the passage of time provides! I handled the whole romantic triangle situation very poorly, to say the least. Rather than stand back with quiet assurance, I let every feeling I had show: in Technicolor® and with Dolby sound. Every conversation contained hidden land mines of emotion—we had to watch every step we took. These loaded talks were not at all conducive to reconciliation. I was possessed by the fear that our wonderful, God-given relationship was crumbling, invaded by an outsider, and I was angered by that reality.

I blamed myself for ignoring to a large degree the needs of our love and now having to pay the price. Alternately, I blamed Tom for not telling me about his new friend, and I raged at him for the indiscretion. In quieter moments I had many high intentions of simply allowing the future to unfold as I prayed and waited patiently. Those times were usually short-lived, though, and my emotions remained raw.

In a positive vein, we constructed a forty-day prayer of

forgiveness which we each extended to one another. This prayer included a specific plea for guidance about our life goals concerning each other. I am sure that our combined efforts at seeking divine intervention were influential in shaping our future together, but the results were not instantaneous. Quite the contrary, we were in for a long haul concerning the healing and rebuilding of our relationship, and in some ways it continues to this day. I was learning how extremely difficult it is for me to let go when it comes to matters of the heart.

Another issue that surfaced radically was my own low self-esteem. I was a twenty-six-year-old woman, not a sixteen-year-old child, yet I was painfully aware of how helpless the situation had left me. I needed only to search for that sixteen year old to discover just how lacking my own sense of self-worth was.

As a teen-ager I was very unathletic in a family of superior athletes. My dad is an excellent golfer, among other things, and my brothers were the stars of their high school football and wrestling teams. Even my mom was an active bowler and golfer. I, however, seemed to never be able to get the ball over the net or into the hoop no matter how hard I tried. It seemed that the more conscious I became of the problem, the worse it was.

If you've never experienced this kind of embarrassment, it might be hard to envision just how personally it affected me. It was excruciating to perform in gym class day after day due to my self-conscious fumbling. It's as if all eyes and spotlights are on you when you are overly aware of yourself, and I compensated by trying to become popular in other ways, which weren't always the most constructive. Being a good student didn't ease my suffering because as a grade schooler my shy, bookish ways went unrewarded by the other kids.

I had forgotten the scared child of yesterday, however,

until this new episode rocked my already unsteady boat. It hurt me more than it should have, and I say that not to deny my own right to feel pain, but because if I had been operating as a whole person, knowing my own true self-worth as a child of God, I would not have felt as destroyed by this event. I know this. In this way the experience was a gift, for I could no longer hide from myself the knowledge that there was work to be done on the little girl I still carried with me, work that could no longer wait.

In the meantime, month after miserable month went by as we made frequent stops and starts together. There were some romantic, intimate moments that would make me feel that all was well with us when blammo! Again the storm would hit. The tug and pulls from another direction would not leave us alone. Finally, after months spent on an emotional roller coaster, the ride ended. I wasn't prepared for the effects our breakup would have on me.

I decided to get away for a while, but I didn't fully realize that I couldn't leave behind the depression or the anxiety that I was experiencing. I drove north to a Chicago suburb where our old matchmaking friend Taras and his wife Donna were home visiting relatives. I hoped that perhaps seeing them would remind me of happier days and somehow convince me that things between Tom and me would eventually work out.

It was Easter weekend, and on Good Friday I decided to drive around the area in hopes of finding a park to sit in in the sunshine and retreat for a while. I was completely unfamiliar with the neighborhoods as I drove aimlessly, with no particular destination in sight. Suddenly, I came upon a convent and pulled in to take a closer look.

There in front of me was a life-sized statue of Saint Francis. Stumbling upon a Franciscan convent was very meaningful to me since Tom and I had met on the feast day of St. Francis, October 4, a fact that I discovered on one of my trips to the chapel of St. Mary's Hospital when I happened upon a bookmark imprinted with the famous prayer attributed to him, as well as an announcement of the approaching feast day. There was renewal in my bones as I sat at the feet of the statue to read from my old friend, *God Calling*.

The combination of sun, quiet, and the words of Jesus were just what I needed to breathe new life into my body, mind, and soul. As I drove away from this peaceful town, with its hills and green trees, my eyes focused on a sign at the side of the road. There, beneath the name of the town, in small letters, was the descriptive phrase "Village of Faith."

Of all the places my wandering car could have led me to, why here? The convent experience would have been quite enough, but what of this additional boost for my weary heart? Was God trying to tell me something? I was just beginning to let go of Tom, why was I now receiving what seemed to me confirmation of the "rightness" of our love? I also wondered if somehow, in my strong yearning to maintain our relationship, I was "conjuring" these happenings through the sheer strength of my desire.

Then again, perhaps I was misreading the meaning behind them. Maybe the convent was merely an attraction for me based upon a prior lifetime spent within the Franciscan order, and seeing "Village of Faith" might have been a reminder to me not to lose mine. I felt so uncertain of everything that was happening, and I did not wish to place my expectations in the wrong direction and be hurt again. My wonderful day faded into a cascade of increasing confusion and doubt.

That night we attended a comedy club, and I found some relief in laughter. Physically, however, I was suffering horribly from cramping that required heavy medication. I was not really paying attention to the amounts I was taking, and the following day I paid a heavy price: twenty-four hours of continuous gastrointestinal upset that kept me in bed. What a guest I was, but my friend's family were wonderful to me, making me soup and providing me with ginger ale to soothe my inflamed stomach lining.

The next day was Easter Sunday, and I set out for home. I had no sooner merged onto the highway when I heard the sweet sounds of Vivaldi's *Four Seasons* playing on the radio. The same sounds that provided me with a background for my affirmations, including the one about attracting a special soul who would love, help, comfort, and bring joy to me—and for whom I would do the same. My eyes blurred a bit as I drove.

At home again, despite being seemingly reinforced in my belief that Tom and I were to someday be together, I decided to make a clean start of my life. For a while I hibernated, surrounded by spiritually uplifting biographies of women with whom I could identify. I read the story of Hannah Whittal Smith, titled *The Unselfishness of God,* and *Hind's Feet on High Places,* Hannah Hurnard's beautifully written allegorical tale of spiritual growth. I tend to retreat into the world of the written word during periods of transition and adjustment. It has always helped me to cope when I am able to identify with the struggles of others, particularly other women, as I find myself again. (Was I identifying with the rejected Hannah of the Bible who bargained with God for a son?)

In time I emerged, hesitantly at first, then with vigor. I dove into conversations in my drama class and finished my English research paper with style and an A+. I was coming alive again; Easter weekend had truly inspired me with Resurrection Power! As time passed, I felt like myself again, only better, and before long someone else noticed my joy.

While browsing one day in my favorite Bible bookstore, I bumped into the cousin of one of my classmates, a tall, handsome man my age. He was a newly "born again" Christian and quickly invited me to services that Wednesday night, to which I just as quickly agreed. That evening began a whirlwind romance that completed the restoration of my war-worn ego. We played guitar and sang gospel tunes together and studied the Bible side by side. His strongly conservative views were different from mine, but I tried to emphasize our agreements instead (this was a mirror of the relationship I had while in Springfield, just before meeting Tom). He was the opposite of Tom, more serious, with a somewhat troubled past. We were each a needed transition for one another, both of us having recently broken long-term relationships.

As is often the case in these "in-between" romances, we weren't destined to be more than a very brief interlude in one another's lives. Tom was once again invading my thoughts, and my friend began dating a girl in the choir. I had tried to convince myself that the time I was spending over the phone with Tom was just indicative of our deep friendship and nothing else, but deep down I'm sure I knew that it was more. It was merely a matter of time before I allowed myself to admit it.

I remember so clearly the night that I began to sense a new beginning was happening for us. We had gone out for burgers when I visited to pick up some paintings he had stored for me. There was a different atmosphere between us, full of the sort of excitement that was there the first time we had met. His eyes seemed much greener than I remembered, and they lit up when he laughed. When he kissed me on the cheek, I felt a twinge of the original spark that had been dormant for so long. Both of us were hesitant to acknowledge what was happening; it was still too soon since our breakup. All ghosts seemed to be gone, and there was only the two of us.

Unfortunately, relationships don't come with a lifetime guarantee. Ours had gone through rough waters indeed, and we each learned that something as special as what we have cannot be ignored. Edgar Cayce said that "love is giving; it is a growth. It may be cultivated or it may be seared." (939-1) We found out almost too late that ours was in need of attention and cultivation, in grave danger of starvation. No one is immune, not even those who are certain that their love is a direct answer to prayer—I learned that the hard way, and I don't intend to forget it. Likewise, spiritual growth doesn't "sleep"; it must be nurtured and brought to full bloom. Unfortunately, some of us think that we can allow it to coast until a need arises, then expect faith to rise up and save us. Not so, and I am living proof of the error in this attitude.

We made our way back together slowly. It wasn't easy. I still had the leftover feelings of resentment to deal with and a healthy self-concept to develop. But our guide was still making contact in the most unusual ways, with unbelievably clever methods of gaining our attention.

As we strolled one evening outside the Union Station in St. Louis, a remodeled mall version of the old train station, a man approached us with a flyer in his hand. We had just ended a discussion about our fear of committing too soon when the little green flyer was thrust into Tom's hand. On the front were the words "Home Sweet Home" and inside a message written by one of the churches which extolled the virtues of married and family life. Tom revealed that he had been praying about the next step we should make together, and with a touch that said he was glad to be back he held me close to him on the crowded walkway.

## 10

# *Heaven on a Sister's Arm*

"When three women join together, the stars come out in broad daylight."  —Taluga Proverb

SELF-CONDEMNATION is probably the ultimate horror that we can inflict on ourselves and one of our most frequent wounds. This type of loathing leads only to disease and broken relationships. The rupture and subsequent healing of my romance with Tom caused red flags to go up in my mind. Despite years of spiritual study and discipline, I was still discounting my incredible significance as a child of God by letting an image of failure tear away my sense of peace. I needed assistance in raising my perception of myself as a woman back to its proper place. The Holy Spirit provided the friends both here and beyond who would help me begin to do that.

How true it is that we attract others to us like magnets, for better or for worse. As a young woman, I shared a common sense of bewilderment that many girls experience. I wasn't sure what I wanted to "do" with my life, and I spent time flailing. My poverty of spirit was attracting me to friends who were mirrors of what I was feeling. I drew a crew of pals who were drifting along, looking for that elusive key to happiness and looking in the places least likely to contain it. There was a sadness inside that was a result of the longing for something that the world couldn't provide.

We tried to ignore the growing suspicion that our unpredictable behavior and risk taking was not leading us where we wanted to go. My short-lived move at age eighteen to Florida with a girlfriend was just one example of a misguided choice. I was miserable, missed my family, and was back within three weeks. It's pure craziness that leads us down these nowhere paths, but without clear signposts it's hard to get off of them.

Being eighteen or even twenty-six and trying to find out who you really are is a trial-by-fire experience. But I'm thankful for the sometimes bumpy ride, because without it I wouldn't understand others when they fall down and need a hand from someone who knows what searching is about. None of us is perfect despite the many masks we wear that pretend we are, and it's time to stop the nonsense of judging and condemning those who have lost their way. I'm also grateful that certain women in my life extended their hands to me.

Startling progress happens when we link our strengths together in an effort to get beyond our individual hang-ups. One sister-friend who has done much to boost my internal image back to a healthy level is my former roommate and fellow nurse, Penny. We met fresh out of nursing school and quickly became pals and sounding boards for one another.

Blonde, with large crystal blue eyes, fair skinned, and several inches taller than me, she is my visual opposite. Our backgrounds were strikingly similar yet vastly different at the same time. Both our fathers work for the same railroad, and each of us is the only girl in the midst of brothers. But Penny had a sheltered upbringing in a small town and a strict Baptist mother. While I didn't have to battle the streets of a city like New York, I hadn't been raised in Mayberry, RFD, either.

Our passion for biscuits and gravy was shared, and I was an impetus for her to get out and let her hair down. We had quiet times of deep conversation as well, and while she credits me with inspiring her back toward an intimate relationship with the Holy Spirit, in truth I needed her presence even more to continue to be "in the world but not of it." When my shaky self-esteem shattered several years after we left our cozy apartment, she was there to help lift me up and out of the darkness.

A friend isn't blind to her beloved's imperfections, but oh how a true one sees past them. What a support Penny was when I was at my weakest, feeling unattractive and unlovable. When we females get caught up in catty competition and back stabbing, we really miss the point. We are here to lean upon each other's arms, to offer that special insight and understanding that only happens woman to woman. As a fellow sufferer struggling to find value within herself, Penny knew what I was feeling and wasn't happy that I was down and out; she instead spoke words I needed to hear and led me away from the pity party.

With a special sensitivity that I've often admired in her, Penny was clear and strong on two points: number one, Tom loves me and always has. She spoke with such authority that I believe it startled both of us. While not always certain about her own relationships, she was completely convinced about mine. Although she wasn't even in the same room with me at the time (she lived in Colorado, while I was in Illinois), I could feel her conviction over the phone.

The second and most important point that she stressed to me was my value as a woman, whether loved by Tom or not. Again, like most of us, she struggles with appreciating herself, but her intensity in insisting that I was O.K. impressed me. It was honest, heartfelt, and greatly needed by me. It wasn't a wishy-washy mumbling of encouragement while mentally reviewing her own plans for later; she was completely present with me, while I bled the final drops of hurt from my soul. I am certain that our mutual Master helped her say the exact words that I needed to hear. He knew she was listening and would share with me what was necessary for my healing.

If I only have one friend such as her in my lifetime, someone willing to listen and be there in my dark valley times, I will have been immeasurably blessed. With the help of Penny and others, I survived my dark night and came out with a heart more tender toward others and the knowing that I really am all right. I forget sometimes, but I have a point of reference to return to that will remind me when I need it. Friends are truly God's wonderful way of showing us more of Himself.

One nice thing about my friendship with Penny is that she isn't hung up on impressing or competing with me. She applauds my successes, but also gives me a kick in the butt when I need it. Because of that I can in turn encourage her, without the hidden fear that she'll "outdo" me or use my weaknesses against me. She is very honest about her struggles, which in turn allows me to show my warts without hesitation. Since neither of us has a biological sister, we fill that role for each other. Just like sisters, we can annoy the heck out of each other from time to time as well. That's the fun of being real.

We cry on each other's shoulders over our men and cuss

them out together, too. I get to hear the latest unfoldments in her relationship with Peter, a friend of Tom's whom I introduced her to, and she gets to listen as I extol both the virtues and downfalls of mine. It's great! Two female minds are always better than one when it comes to unraveling the mysteries of romantic entanglements. We were born only five days apart, so now we can also explore what it means to be thirty-something together.

I always said and believed from the time I was a teenager that my thirties would begin the most secure and probably happiest time of my life. Why? Because I knew that given enough time and experience, I would overcome my self-conscious fears and learn to be myself in a strong and life-affirming way. Well, I'm now there—in my thirties, that is—and while I was right about the incredible changes that have occurred in my mind and heart, I still have a long way to go. Now I'm championing my fortieth decade. I know that it's going to be an awesome period in my life, especially with good friends like Penny around to share it with.

Along with the flesh and blood support that Penny has given in my journey toward appreciation of myself, there were examples brought to my attention of those who walked a foreign land two thousand years ago. Women the Master knew.

In Jesus' time women were not revered, but He sought to change that. His closest companions were often female, and women held positions of power in that early movement. It was many years later that a patriarchal order was hoisted back in place. Christ taught that men and women are equal before God, and, contrary to His teaching, others, even the apostle Paul, sometimes preached male superiority. Still, Paul had as his first convert, Lydia, and Priscilla became a leader in the church of Corinth and later at Ephesus an outspoken orator, with his full support.

Having someone believe in you and support you in all

you try to accomplish is the miracle of love. We might not always agree, but if we try to listen with an open mind and heart to one another, our world expands. These New Testament visionaries came alive for me as I studied. They provided strong models for me to aspire to, and I could almost feel their presence in the room with me when I read their stories.

The women of biblical times were not the sanitized people I once envisioned when I thought of them through churchified eyes. Jesus was considered a devil by the conservative religious leaders of His time. He told His followers that if He was considered Beelzebub, how much more so would the people of His household be condemned as such (Matthew 10:25). Those who chose to follow His teachings were in danger of losing their lives, not to mention their reputations. They weren't home spinning wool and baking cakes without a concern in their pretty little heads. Isn't it much the same today when we follow the guidance of the spirit that is sometimes in contradiction with the common sense of the rest of the world? Sometimes we're asked to do things that appear crazy to others, and it takes guts to follow through. If those ladies could do it with the help of the Father and each other, so can we!

Claudia Procula, the wife of Pilate, has a story that intrigues and inspires. Some believe she may have been a secret follower of Jesus, and the Greek Orthodox church canonized her and has designated October 27 as her feast day. This brave woman sent a message to her husband by a servant, as recorded in Matthew:

> "When he [Pilate] was set down on the judgment seat, his wife sent unto him, saying, Have thou nothing to do with that just man: for I have suffered many things this day in a dream because of him." (Matthew 27:19)

Pilate was influenced by the crowds, however, who shouted, "Crucify Him!" and he chose to ignore her warning out of fear of them. Her dream warned not only that Jesus was innocent, but that Pilate would suffer because of it. Though he acquitted Jesus and proclaimed that he had found no fault with Him, his administration ended abruptly and he purportedly was banished to France. He later ended his life in suicide, according to some sources.

But Claudia did her part by heeding the voice of the spirit, which revealed itself in her dream, despite the fact that Jesus was so despised by the religious leaders and now even the common people had turned against Him. Sometimes the inner spirit is so compelling that it would be far more uncomfortable to go against it than with it, and we do so with spunk in the face of all naysayers. Certainly this is what Pilate's wife felt that darkened day.

I am fired up by the knowledge that our heritage is strong and a cause for celebration. I wrongly denigrated myself when I lived in a place of loathing, and the sisterhood was showing me that it is my duty to carry on in their courageous footsteps. How often had I ignored the voice of Spirit out of fear? It is time to end that trend and live as a female warrior. I have to remind myself of my rightful place in God's plans many times; but with His help and the hand of my friends, I am able to stand again—even stronger—after each fall.

# 11

## *Without Bounds*

> "Love is the voice under all silences,
> the hope which has no opposite in fear;
> the strength so strong mere force is feebleness:
> the truth more first than sun more last than star."
> —e.e. cummings

LOVE is seldom simple. I was urged by my Master, that quiet day by the lake, to learn to love unconditionally and was given an indication of how it could be done. Jesus promised that spending time with Him is key to my learning the art of loving. I've found that to be true, and I've also cherished the introductions He makes for me to people who model the way of love in such a fashion that there is no doubt that He has touched them. While rebuilding my relationship with Tom, I was given a moving example of true love between a man and a woman in action, a lesson in love without bounds.

My white cap and gold pin have led me into the lives of

many people whom I might otherwise never have met. It is the highest honor to be allowed the privilege of serving in this manner. Most often I find myself receiving gifts from those I am entrusted to assist that are far greater than anything I could give. Suffering seems to produce a more acute sense of the fragility of the physical body and a realization of how fleeting our time here on earth is. With it comes a certain peace and appreciation for life which those of us who rush through our days often miss. In the summer of 1990 I met a man who shared this truth with me.

Henry is a rugged man. He worked the riverboats on the Mississippi at a very early age, having left school to make his own way in the world. Tall, broad shouldered, large of body and of heart. "Red" was his nickname in the early years, earned because of his thick, red hair. Cautiously fearless, he made his presence known on the streets of St. Louis, where he grew up. The many stories he shared with me made it clear that he has always been a bit of a renegade, with a thirst for adventure.

The woman who would become his "bride," as he lovingly refers to her, was a sweet Catholic girl named Micki. Her infinite patience in allowing him room to express his wild side only served to make him love her more. They married when Henry realized he never wanted to be without her, and soon two girls and a boy joined their home.

He often joked with me that while he loves his children beyond words, it is his wife whom he chose as his partner in life, and she comes first! Truly theirs are two hearts and souls knit together. By the time I met him, their marriage exceeded thirty years, and there was no evidence of the bitterness or indifference that can grow over a period of years together. They were not saintly or unearthly either; they had their battles just as all normal couples do. The disagreements seemed to me to be in the present, however, not a rehashing of long ago events.

Eventually Henry began working with explosives, using dynamite to clear the way for roads to be built in the Missouri landscape. From there a position in construction evolved, and one summer he supervised the building of an overlay on the St. Louis Lambert Airport runway that would succeed in giving it international status.

One hot morning in August as he prepared for another day's work, Micki urged him to stay at home. There were dark and heavy rain clouds in the sky, and she was uncomfortable with his leaving. As they stood saying their goodbys, Henry reassured her by predicting an early knock-off from work that day, since rain looked inevitable. They kissed and hugged as usual, then he drove away.

She went about her housework, still a bit uneasy. There were many times when Henry had been in danger, and she had sensed it correctly. Once he was many miles away, and she was at home with a relative who was staying overnight. She awoke in fear, waiting for the phone to ring, and when it did, it was a hospital worker informing her that he had just been in a serious accident that left him with a broken back. That was just one of many incidents that revealed a connection that went beyond physical limitations.

Her thoughts were interrupted when the phone shrieked through her reverie once again, bringing news that would change her life irrevocably. There had been an accident at the airport. Her husband, whom she had shared breakfast with only hours earlier, had been trapped beneath a massive, cement-hauling truck! An ambulance carried him to a nearby hospital in critical condition. She rushed in a daze to be by his side.

That accident happened on August 5, 1981. He spent the next ninety days strapped onto a rotating "Roto-Kinetic" bed: a quadriplegic permanently paralyzed from the neck down. Fortunately, the injury occurred at a level of his spinal cord that did not render him ventilator dependent, meaning he would be able to breathe on his own. After eleven months in the hospital learning to function with his new limitations, he returned home. The ordeal had peeled 100 pounds from his 220-pound frame. Able to breathe and move his arms, but not to use his fingers or legs. Something which, unless you have been paralyzed yourself, cannot be even dimly realized.

I've tried imagining a tickle on the side of my face or any other body part for that matter. It grows from mild annoyance to an overwhelming urge to dig the nails in and SCRATCH! Only, I'm not able to reach up to alleviate the irritating itchiness. I've attempted to envision the helplessness of being unable to go to the bathroom on my own and having to rely instead on tubes inserted by someone else to intermittently empty my bladder. Sometimes, as I've gone through my day, I've stopped to consider what life without the use of my legs or fingers would be like for every minor and major movement required in living. I can't, really; it's something that can only be guessed at.

I've assisted in the care of other men who have suffered paralysis, some from only the waist down, with full use of their upper bodies. There is a very understandable possibility for becoming full of bitterness at a loss of function so devastating, and some are. Not so with Henry. He carried the same stubbornness and strength of spirit of the cocky, confident man on the street into his new life in a wheelchair. While his body lives with an impairment that drastically changed life as he knew it, his mind has compensated with a freedom of thought and intelligence that I've not often witnessed.

To think I came so close to not meeting this incredible man. The nursing agency asked if I would take this homecare case in Eureka, thirty miles from my apartment in St. Louis, where I was living near Tom after we made it through the rough times of our breakup. I didn't want to drive that far, and I was a bit tired of home care and wanted to continue the hospital work I was doing. When they called in July to beg me to go, I was ready to say no. They offered me twice my wages if I would work just two twelve-hour shifts over a weekend, so I agreed, believing I wouldn't go back. Once again I owe a debt of gratitude to my guide for leading me there.

Henry was so easy to be with, hilarious and kind, that I knew I couldn't stay away. By the end of that first weekend, I signed on to work full-time with him. His affectionate nickname for me became "Decatur," after my hometown. With a permanent confusion about whether my boyfriend's name was Tony or Tom, he simply combined the two. Every evening one of the first things he would ask is, "How's Tony-Tom?" I was soon to learn that this man has an unsurpassed gift of gab, with a never-ending supply of jokes and stories that have kept friends returning for years.

Nine years had passed since his injury, and he freely spoke of that gray day. He insisted he harbored no hatred for the man who had accidentally run over him, philosophizing that in the life he had lived, danger was a constant threat, and tragedies were bound to happen. For a man with such a natural tendency to love and laugh, resentment would have been the *coup de grâce* after the accident plowed through his life.

All of this is not to say he had a sweet, everything's O.K., Pollyanna attitude toward the losses he suffered. There was pain, and I'm positive it went deeper than I'll ever be able to know. Especially when it came to Micki, his bride, the love of his life. We spoke about his feelings for her one late night. She was away on a trip, and the faraway look in his eyes gave me the feeling that he was not fully present with me either. He spoke of his longing to have her near him at night again, instead of being confined to a hospital-style bed with a nurse nearby. It touched me that he trusted me enough to share this ache.

His mind and heart seemed to be connected to her, wherever she was. Whenever I observed them together, I marveled at the tenderness between them. She was his constant champion and helpmate. I told him of my bottom-of-my-heart conviction that this hardship was temporary, that they would be together in a complete way once again. He seemed to lift a bit from his sadness and echoed my thoughts. He proclaimed that there was no doubt that one day he would dance with her again, whether it be in another life or somewhere on the other side of the thin veil that separates us from our true home. For a moment, we stepped outside of time. It was magic.

His ability to transcend time was apparent to me from the beginning. Shower nights were always an ordeal for him. It meant retiring early from his family to undergo several hours of personal care. Throughout all the procedures and rituals, he told stories from his life. Detailed, highly entertaining events that he had experienced. This focus on anecdote helped him separate a bit from the unpleasant aspects of his physical care. I often thought that he was more present in those escapades than in current time, and I was lucky to travel there with him.

I walked the construction sites of years ago with him and learned a little about the art of using dynamite. With edge-of-the-seat anticipation, I listened as he relived tangles with the law—he was never one to back down from a fight.

Always there, despite the circumstances, is an irresistible happiness. Henry refuses to let conditions determine his attitude. A man strong, healthy, enormously independent and fearless now had to rely on others for even the simplest of functions. Yet he can laugh and often has everyone around him in stitches. And it is Henry who takes part in the management of his disability, just as any true leader would, devising time-saving methods and creative alternatives to the usual "nursey" interventions. He even drove his own van for a time, despite being able to only barely move his hands and remaining devoid of finger manipulation.

It proved to me beyond a shadow of a doubt that true strength is not a result of brawn; rather, it is a function of the spirit. When I look at him, I forget about his disability, because even with the wheelchair staring back at me I see something else. I see one of the most forceful and resolute men I know using his mind and heart to help himself and those he loves.

He once told me that if he could have the use of his legs again for just one day, he would choose to take a walk through the woods with Micki. Years of camping and fishing trips had made him a lover of the outdoors. He explained that he wouldn't want to do anything that would only make him miss it more afterward, but a walk among the trees one more time would do his spirit good. We sat together in the crisp Missouri air with the hills surrounding us as we spoke. The feeling was not one of depressed sentimentality, but of a hopeful, anything's possible yearning. I always felt this excitement when I was with Henry. Tragedy and loss cannot take away a person's innate belief in the miracle of life. His curiosity and love of discovery carried infectious optimism.

Becoming another person's hands and legs produces a closeness that is hard to describe. I feel that I couldn't love Henry any more than if he were a part of my blood line. He is connected to me by bonds much deeper than mere red and white cells! He reminds me of my dad in many ways, with similar attitudes, likes and dislikes. Henry enjoys watching cop shows on television, and he knows an automobile inside and out, just like my dad. As he gets to know the nurses who have necessarily invaded his life, he begins to care for them the way a father does. And a father's love is unconditional.

In general we learn through example. A child emulates

parents; teen-agers follow the lead of their peers. Watching Henry and Micki love and accept his circumstances in joyful creativity was a classroom experience *par excellence* for me. We were together for just over a year. When it was time to move on, it was difficult for me to let go. Our last night together (I worked the 7:00 p.m. to 7:00 a.m shift) found me painfully aware of the end of another chapter in my life. A chapter gloriously written in by my God.

We went about our usual schedule, trying to dismiss feelings of impending separation from our minds. Always just before turning out the lights, I would sit by his bed feeding him crackers and peanut butter while watching car chases or science fiction fantasy on television. It was getting quite late, and we couldn't seem to bring ourselves to turn off the set. Henry turned to me and with tears in his eyes said "Decatur, I just don't want to go to sleep tonight, because I know you're not coming back. I wish the night didn't have to end." I assured him I would be back for visits and tried to believe that nothing was changing. I knew if I allowed myself one teardrop, there would be no holding back the flow.

Tears would come later and along with them a smile that starts in the pit of my heart and spills into the corners of my room. Henry helped lead me deeper into the reality of love's presence and made loving a much simpler proposition for me.

*Four days after this manuscript was completed, Henry died. The day was Saturday, December 4, 1993.*

My friend, I salute you. I raise my glass and utter a prayer of blessing and thanks for having known you. I smile as I remember you. I celebrate your freedom and mourn your temporary physical separation from those you love so much. I extend my love, and hope (know) that we will one day meet again.

# *12*

# *Moving Mountains*

> "It is one of the most beautiful compensations of this life that no man can sincerely try to help another without helping himself."
> —Ralph Waldo Emerson

HUMAN guides such as Henry, who show the way through their gallant example, are potent agents for changing our usual limited thinking. Hopelessness can be such an alluring and comfortable feeling to sink into that it often takes great effort to choose faith instead. Believing can be scary, with the threat of a letdown looming over one's head. But collectively, the power of hope and the affirmation that "It is well" can move powerful pillars of negative circumstance. Once again, I needed a flesh-and-blood example to keep my feet planted where God needed them to be—in faith.

I reported to work that afternoon expecting nothing

greatly out of the ordinary, although in nursing there are never guarantees. I was working in an intensive care (ICU) "step down" unit, which meant that our patients were still too ill for a general medical floor, but not critical enough for the close watch of ICU. When I approached the nurse's station, the supervisor directed me to intensive care instead. They were short of help, and I would work there for the evening since it was my turn to "float." This prospect didn't thrill me. It's always unsettling to go to another area, away from one's own comfort zone.

I began to receive a report from the nurse in charge when the supervisor joined us. She explained that since I hadn't received an orientation to her unit, I didn't have to stay if I didn't want to. I agreed to stay unless someone were willing to trade with me. She laughed and commented on my "diplomacy," and for a moment I kicked myself for not jumping at the chance to leave while it was available. The supervisor determined that a quick in-service to the area would suffice, and then I would help out wherever needed, rather than being assigned specific patients.

The report resumed, and I learned that a critically ill trauma victim was receiving one-on-one care, and I would probably not have to assist unless things got too hectic for his private nurse. It seemed that he had fallen many feet from a roof, sustaining a massive head injury, and wasn't expected to live through the night. I noted his young age, thirty-three, the same as my brother's. Then I finished taking my notes before beginning the daily rounds of vital signs and assessments.

An hour or two into the shift, I sat making notations in a chart when my eye caught the family surrounding the man unconscious in bed, ventilator performing his respirations, head wrapped in bandages. Familiarity began to creep into my awareness, and I grabbed his chart with heart pounding. Shock spread throughout my body as I realized that this "hopeless case" was a man I'd known all my life! He had grown up three houses down from us and graduated from high school with my oldest brother. I was suddenly numb.

His condition was so grave that a permit for organ donation was already in place and plans for removing the ventilator were in progress. I watched as his wife stood by the bed crying and holding his hand, and thought of his young children at home. It's always much more jarring when tragedy hits so close. In stunned silence, I approached his room.

His mother and father looked haggard, as though a thousand years had been compressed into one day. When they recognized me, I saw a bit of relief in their eyes that something familiar had been added to this hellish and unknown journey that involved innumerable hospital devices so foreign to the average person. Their beloved son lay dying as tubes and machines horrifically buzzed and hummed, and the helplessness in their faces was shattering. They shared with me information about his accident and reaffirmed their belief that the prayers going out for him were powerful and that the situation was not hopeless in their minds. I felt optimistic in talking with them; there was a definite spirit of faith in that cramped room. I offered my prayers as well, and they genuinely thanked me.

I finished the rest of the workday in a daze. At home that night, I thought about what had occurred. As I stood showering, I prayed with all the intensity of concentration that I could summon. With the warm water streaming over me, I entered a state of heightened attention in prayer. This was no quick mumbling of blessing. It was a strong desire for God's will to be done expressed in thanksgiving and love.

Meredith Puryear, in her book *Healing Through Meditation and Prayer*, explains why it is imperative that we be careful how we pray for those who haven't requested it themselves. We are not able to "surrender" to God for another person, but that doesn't prevent us from being of help.

Puryear lists four criteria to consider when determining how to be of assistance to another: Do what is at hand, do what we are drawn to do by our hearts, do that which we choose with our minds to do, and finally do that which is in keeping with the ideals and purposes of the soul, always leaving the increase or the results in God's hands. (p. 48) Prayer is powerful and creative in and of itself. It can become witchery if done without regard to the will of both the individual and the Creator. I knew that this man lying in the hospital was a deeply spiritual person. I felt the strong drive to pray for the awareness of the presence of God (for He is never absent; it is only our ability to perceive Him that is lacking) to be with him and with all who cared about him.

Back at work the following day I learned with relief that my former neighbor had made it through the night. Additional family members had flown in from around the country and were keeping vigil. I spoke with his wife during my dinner break and learned that she was not about to give up on her man. I was impressed as I looked into her clear and determined eyes to see such unwavering faith. Others around her did not seem as unshakably optimistic, yet were struggling to be positive. She was also angry, and let it show. Her anger was for those who continually found it their duty to "prepare her for the worst." She told me she had asked the doctor on the case not to give her any more negative promises, because she expected a miracle.

From the brain waves and other tests it appeared that she was simply denying the inevitable, because there were ominous signs that seemed to guarantee either death or life as a vegetable for this man. But day after day he showed small signs of improvement, as day after day we prayed.

Since I was working only part-time while attending school full-time, several days passed without my seeing the family, yet they were close to my mind and heart as I went about my own hectic life. I was in for a shock when I finally returned to the hospital. There on my "step down" unit, fully awake and fairly alert, was the "hopeless case"! Free of the extensive monitoring devices that invaded him from limb to limb, breathing independently. Speaking, although with some difficulty in matching the appropriate words with thoughts; smiling and overflowing with gratitude at being alive.

I was amazed. Me, who believes in miracles and the reality of the transforming power of prayer. It's just that I hadn't often seen the results "close up" and in such an indisputable way. I absolutely tingled at the magnitude of the whole experience. I don't remember the rest of the evening, but I spent many shifts marveling as his complete recovery unfolded. Today he enjoys a full life, back at work and with his family.

I thought about the afternoon I reported to the ICU. If I had forced my way, I could have been dismissed from the unit and sent back to the security blanket of my own area. Luckily, I had begun to learn that being a servant means being willing to go wherever God sends me. How often had I repeated the affirmation in my Search for God group, "... as the call comes, 'Here am I, send me, use me' "? (262-3) The real meaning of that vow becomes clear when plans topple, and I'm asked to abandon my will for a greater one. I don't always choose the way that I know is in line with my ideal, but this time I did. If I hadn't, I'd have missed the opportunity to take part in a drama of the utmost importance, to lend my prayers to the wave of those already being offered.

No, God didn't lead me there because my prayers are somehow advanced or different. I stumble along like everyone else. Rather, I was allowed the privilege and honor of being included in a mass appeal of love and faith that would teach and strengthen myself and all those involved.

The man in the bed with the many tubes in place was a

gift to us all, an experience in faith. I am thankful to him. I know that if ever I am faced with a similar circumstance, I have within me an additional capacity to conquer the fear that can drown a person, and I owe it to his suffering and survival. The "knowing" within me grew a little more, and I am changed by my encounter with courage and belief at the height of a storm.

Always questioning, I stood back from this incident pondering the old mystery of why prayer is necessary. Doesn't God know what we need and just take care of it? I don't believe in begging (although I do it from time to time!), so what is the purpose of continual prayer and concern? If I'm honest with myself, I know that I need to examine my concept of who God is and perhaps abandon some long-held childish renditions of Him that make Him over in my image. It's supposed to be the other way around. After all, God made us in His likeness. The readings say that we are to be "co-creators with God." Jesus said in the Gospel of John 14:20:

> At that day ye shall know that I am in my Father, and ye in me, and I in you.

This oneness is taught in the readings and is the basis for understanding prayer. Again, to paraphrase Meredith Puryear, the love and blessings God has to offer are already there, we are not trying to twist His arm into unleashing power that He'd rather keep to Himself. Prayer simply helps to make the connections crucial to bringing into our awareness the energy of His love. We help others to become open and receptive to this vast help available to all. I have to remind myself continually that we live, move, and have our being in Him. We're not separate; we're connected, as Jesus said, and sometimes we have to give it all we've got to help others remove the scales from their eyes and in the process our sight clears as well.

Sometimes our prayers may help someone make the transition to the other side, and that's O.K. Death heals, too. In my early years as a nurse I was lucky enough to work with a woman who knew this fact very well: my old friend and Therapeutic Touch counterpart. I stood with Virginia as she helped an old and tired woman let go and enter the light of God's love. The patient was dying of terminal cancer and had lingered for several days at the brink of death. One night we entered her room to find her barely able to breathe, struggling to maintain a weak grasp on life. Holding her hand and speaking softly, Virginia comforted and urged her not to be afraid, and we prayed as this one quietly made her exit. I was moved by the intensity of my mentor's caring and concern. She shaped my vision of nursing in many ways, and I am forever indebted.

Over and over we have heard the story of Jesus telling His disciples that their faith need only be as a "grain of mustard seed" in order to move mountains. How much more powerful an analogy could the Master produce than the visual images of a tiny seed and a massive rock. Faith is palpable; it moves the earth. It is not simply a word on a page signifying holy allegiance. *A Search for God*, Book I, states: "Man's divine privilege is to accept, use, develop, and enjoy the fruits of faith." (p. 43)

If a seed can move mountains, imagine what a speck can do. A flicker of faith can renew, redesign, and replenish every area of our lives. If only the true magnitude of Jesus' words would dawn upon us all, we would be instantly healed of our collective insanity. Love would overrule our fright, and hopelessness would disappear.

Incidents such as my encounter in the hospital with my neighborhood friend did much to ripen the fruits of my faith—to bring sanity to my sometimes crazy world and give me hope. A hope that was leading me joyfully to some of the major milestones in my life.

## 13

## *Dew upon the Flower*

> "... I will give them one heart ... I will be their God."  —Ezekiel 11:19-20

JANUARY in Florida is a gift. A wonderland of sun and sea breezes that can lift away a Northerners' light-deprived doldrums. I am no exception. Tom's first winter there helped me realize that the thick layers of ice we had battled in our streets the previous year were quite a weighty disadvantage for the North. Also, family would be more likely to visit and escape the harsh winds, especially my golf-loving mom and dad. The case for the South was slowly gaining an edge, as Tom worked at persuading me to settle there.

We had become engaged two years earlier, right after my January birthday, but hadn't sailed easily into matrimonial bliss. Many years spent in nomadic style had left me feeling the desire to stay put. I loved St. Louis and being close enough to see my family whenever I wanted. So when Tom seemed to have his heart set on the warmer air of Florida, I resisted. I pulled away, as mixed emotions flooded my soul. I decided to stay behind and give myself time to find out if my reservations would pass.

He vacillated between wanting to stay and feeling pulled to go; finally wanderlust won. With two cars and a U-Haul® truck, we transported his things to Florida. He drove me back a few weeks later, and my heart was heavy. For the next few days we became each other's shadow. When I wasn't working, we went everywhere together. The thought of being apart again suddenly seemed unbearable. I was leaving for work the night he left, and when I returned home the next morning, my world seemed much smaller. I played the message he had left on my machine, letting me know when he had gotten on the road, and I couldn't stop the tears. We had been through so much, and now another "opportunity" had arrived. I wondered how much more we could take.

Once again we began a long-distance relationship filled with lengthy phone calls, interspersed with the silence that eight hundred miles brings. He visited St. Louis; I had prolonged stays in Jacksonville. Finally, it was more than we could stand.

We had lingered at the edge long enough and were tired of simply testing the waters. In January, five months after his initial move to Florida, we decided upon a summertime wedding, allowing just six months to plan and organize the many details of a traditional ceremony.

For me it is a ritual steeped in meaning and filled with purpose. It does not just produce a "piece of paper" that adds nothing to a commitment. The promising declarations made before God and others actually change the two. Throughout mine I made plans for frequent readings and songs that actually put into words the belief that "the two shall become one." Drs. Bill and Gladys McGarey noted in their book *There Will Your Heart Be Also: Edgar Cayce's Readings About Home and Marriage:*

> We cannot conceive of man as a spiritual being and yet dismiss a physical act, a signed agreement, or a law as being simply physical and no more. It has more ramifications than that. It concerns the whole being of the persons involved, their relationship to each other, to others, and to God. So the signing of a marriage license has deep significance. When a couple decides to live together without an outer manifestation of marriage, they miss something inside themselves. (p. 75)

To me, that idea does not imply moral judgment, but is simply an affirmation of the belief that letting our voices be heard in the "I do!" that marriage brings is a strong and mystical act. The whole idea of "joining hearts" has always intrigued me. Cayce frequently described marriage partners as ideally being complements to one another. I believe this is a clue to the mystery of becoming one. There is a oneness among all people, but in marriage two people combine their talents, strengths, weaknesses, and everything else that makes them unique to fuse into something new. While retaining individuality, each somehow becomes "more." Uniting with another person in this way does not mean that either one is incomplete without the other, merely that there has been a conscious decision to allow themselves to participate in a wild act of synergism.

With these visions of the grand possibilities it would open for us, I began the necessary decision making for the big day. Royal blue, liquid satin for my bridesmaids; basic black tuxedos for the men; simple, pink silk roses for all; a straight white, off-the-shoulder beaded gown for me. Part of the fun of planning a wedding is the togetherness the bride-to-be has with her excited friends and family. My mom was fabulous as a helper, never demanding, always supportive and encouraging. We shopped all over for her dress and ended up finding a beautiful pale blue peplum style with rhinestone-lined buttons right at home in Decatur! Lots of exciting, playful days spent shopping and joking, having lunch in little diners along the highway on the way to and from St. Louis. Forever memories.

We chose to have a small wedding party: my sister-in-law, Kay, as matron of honor; my two best friends, Denise and Penny, as bridesmaids. Our entire wedding party except for Kay and myself had to fly in for the wedding, and we didn't want to make it any more complicated than it already was. My girls were wonderful, surprising me with special gifts and playful times. Denise kept her St. Louis apartment open to me for all of my trips to the bridal store during my dress fittings. Delicious Mexican meals and endless girl talk. She and I and Rachel, one of my Scripture readers, had dinner in a sort of minibachelorette party. They both lived two hours away from me; it was a way to celebrate since getting everyone together at once would be difficult. They are my adopted sisters, and I love them dearly.

Trips to Florida involved working with a local Irish-Catholic priest who handled the paperwork for us. The three of us enjoyed a laugh when, in response to his question about whether or not we would raise our kids Catholic, Tom irresistibly explored the idea of "experimenting" by trying a different religion with each child. Luckily, Father Logan had an Irish sense of humor.

A year and a half earlier, following our engagement, we participated in a weekend "engaged encounter" sponsored by the church. It was much more than I expected. Married couples shared honest, sometimes painful anecdotes from their lives together about such issues as finance, child rearing, and sex. The priest leading the retreat even opened up to talk about his falling in love with a close friend and married woman. He told of the difficulty he had in choosing to walk away from incredibly strong emotions and remain true to his vows. I felt deeply for him and respected his honesty and ability to let down the mask of ecclesiastic pomp that sometimes separates clergy from the rest of the world. After each session we engaged couples parted for a time to write out our thoughts about the discussion and the questions provided us.

We laughed, argued, made up, and found a few unexpected discoveries during that Friday through Sunday marathon. No telephones, television, or outside interference for two whole days. I think it should be a yearly requirement for maintaining a marriage license. After all, doctors and nurses must have many hours of continuing education each year, and marriage can be much trickier than medicine.

At the end of the weekend, a communion service provided each person the opportunity to read aloud a message for their partner. It was surprising to hear shy men really revealing themselves and the love they had for their ladies, for God and all to hear. The Cayce material suggested setting ideals, writing down on paper the force that each would have guide their decisions in life. The encounter weekend was, in a sense, a way of doing just that. The questions we focused on forced us to look within for answers we might not have given much thought to before. They allowed us to go beyond the whirl that the outer trappings of marriage planning entail, to the issues that would face us when the rice settled and the guests drove away.

We explored the concept of being "life-giving" or, in other words, constructive and helpful to one another. We considered specific ways that we are life-giving in our relationship:

during decision making, in times of jealousy, when choosing to make love. I liked this approach, with an emphasis on love as a choice and not always a feeling. It is when the other person has been most annoying or has betrayed us in some way that the effort to give life rather than tear it down is essential to practicing the way of love. This kind of love requires letting go of the need to control and "get even," and allowing God to intervene in the situation. Oh, how I need a daily reminder of this and how thankful I am for the experience of affirming this as our ideal in married life together!

It was fortunate that we had completed our engaged encounter so early (a requirement of the Catholic church), because Tom's first year in practice was far too busy to allow for the getaway. There was barely time to discuss such far-reaching matters as our first dance song (which we had difficulty agreeing on—he kept insisting on "Muskrat Love" as a joke—aye)! Also, the myriad preparatory details could not deter us since we had not yet set a date at the time we participated in the retreat. It gave us the chance to work through some of the blocks we had been confronting in our life together before progressing to catering decisions. Now our minds could focus on the matter at hand, as we saw to the business of creating seating arrangements.

I wanted my nephews to have a part in the ceremony, and all agreed but the oldest, who had become a teen-ager not too eager to have the spotlight thrown on him. Jeff and Tim, the two middle boys, would read from the Song of Solomon:

> For, lo, the winter is past, the rain is over and gone; The flowers appear on the earth; the time of the singing of birds is come... (2:11-12)

This was a favorite of mine and signified the new beginning we would be making. Also, it was brief and would not add to the burden of memorization for them on an already hectic day.

Jason, the baby of the family, now a mature seven years old, had agreed to the important job of ring bearer, as long as he wouldn't have to march down the aisle with the dreaded female. Since I really had no little girls that I was close to anyway, I decided to forego having a flower girl.

Rachel, my good friend whom I had met while living in St. Louis and with whom I had made a trip to Virginia Beach the year before, would be reading the love chapter in I Corinthians. Paul's passionate insistence that love is patient, kind, not easily hurt or offended, and quick to forgive is advice we all need branded into our minds when we marry.

It had been a long courtship for us, filled with highs and lows, and now that we had come to this moment in time, it was imperative to bring as much positive affirmation of love into the Mass as possible to celebrate the survival of ours. I wrote a message that I had imprinted in the wedding program. It went like this:

> We would like to give our thanks to each one of you for being here to share in our joy and excitement. Thank you for being a part of our special day, a day of both covenant and laughter.
>
> Our hearts are full as we also thank our parents for their love and support always, under all conditions. We love you more than words can express.
>
> May we also pause to thank the One who brought us together and who has kept us together through seemingly impossible (never say that word) circumstances, our Lord and best Friend, Jesus Christ.
>
> With all of our love,<br>Carolyn and Tom

Like the person who appreciates life much more having faced catastrophic illness, surviving the conflicts inevitable in a relationship makes the culmination in a day of union much more valuable to the two who endured. Our preparations continued in gladness and with great anticipation. Finally, the week of the wedding arrived.

Tom and his mother reached the Midwest together on Wednesday evening. She had flown to Florida a week earlier to prepare the apartment for my arrival. Her thoughtfulness helped make my first taste of married life sweet. Their flight overbooked due to the ticketing wars, so they landed in St. Louis with no connecting flight available to Decatur. My dad and I made the trip to pick them up, and my heart fell when I saw them coming down the ramp—they both looked thoroughly exhausted. It was after midnight when we got home and checked them into the hotel for a much overdue rest.

The following two days were a whirlwind of activity: marriage license, tuxedo fittings, and the arrival of our bridal party, family, and friends from New York, Florida, Georgia, Minnesota, Missouri, Wisconsin, Ohio, as well as various parts of Illinois. On Thursday evening we gathered at my parents' home for my mom's famous thin-sliced roast beef, then on to our respective bachelor and bachelorette parties. I was beginning to show signs of nervousness.

Friday night brought rehearsal in the large, cathedral-style church of St. Patrick's. The priest was someone I had recently met, a young man my age, full of jokes and chuckles. Afterward, we all gathered in an intimate room at the Blue Mill restaurant for a wonderful meal. My other sweetheart, my nephew Jeff, quickly took a seat next to me on my right and told his dad in very clear terms that this was where he would stay.

The grilled fish and twice-baked potato were delicious,

but for once in my life it was difficult to eat due to my excitement. Tom's groomsman, a medical school buddy and boyfriend of my bridesmaid, Penny, got more jovial than most. When I exited the restroom, there was Peter, standing atop a chair with Polaroid® in hand, ready to snap the bride-to-be's picture! I thought it was a hilarious stress-buster, and it helped take my mind off such things as seating arrangements for a moment.

Back at the hotel, friends had begun to congregate, and in the lounge I happily greeted the Milwaukee brothers, whom I'd met in Virginia Beach. Tom's St. Louis Jewish Hospital co-workers were starting to party, and we sat for a while to catch up. Unfortunately, the night had to end early due to the 9:00 a.m. photo session the next day. The minutes were ticking by quickly.

Back at home, in my bed for my last night as a single woman, I couldn't sleep. The usual milk and Tylenol® didn't help, neither did warm chamomile tea. My mind was racing and wouldn't slow down. My prayers helped calm me a little, but not for long. Eventually I drifted into a light sleep, but a couple of hours later a voiceless phone call destroyed any hope of it lasting. I arose at 7:00 to begin preparations.

Light make-up, a few sweeps with the curling iron to my shoulder length hair, and I was ready. I still couldn't eat; I was too manic. My dad kept reassuring me and saying things like, "You've done a great job planning this wedding. Everything's going to be fine." His well-hidden nervousness displayed itself when he forgot the button covers for his shirt. The two of us drove together to the church and just ahead of us was Tom driving my car, my instructions to him to arrive early for pictures forgotten. The photographer, prepared for tardiness, managed to see to it that we finished with time to spare.

Then, there I was, lined up at the back of the church with Jason, my dad, Kay, and my bridesmaids. The organist played the first few beautiful strains of "Jesu Joy of Man's Desiring," and the party members began their entrance. Slowly they walked the long aisle to form a line at the front of the church. With a sudden surge the powerful notes of "Trumpet Voluntary" signaled me to begin my walk. Arm in arm, my dad and I took the steps leading to the altar.

Words of love, commitment, and songs of joy filled the church. Vows, those mysterious connecting promises that change two people forever, were said aloud. Family joined in prayer and in my favorite hymn, "Be Not Afraid." The air filled with the magic of a fairy tale come true. The beast that had taunted us, known for his fear, uncertainty, and distrust, transformed into a prince bringing peace, faith, and conviction in a love that lasts.

We turned to face the congregation, meeting the smiles of those closest to us. Each of us changed, enhanced by the melding process we had just participated in. I can't say I felt different in any highly discernible way. It's similar to being asked if you feel older when the day of your birthday arrives. Noting the day on the calendar there is awareness that another year has past, but the changes were small and imperceptible over time. We had begun this process that October day in 1985, and this event was a culmination of the nearly seven years that had passed since then. The ceremony merely sealed the pact we had made and allowed us to take another step in our climb together. We were both aware of the highly charged emotion in the room and in ourselves, as we made our walk up the aisle as Dr. and Mrs. Murray!

The time for cutting loose came at the reception. At the end of a well-done toast, Tom's brother and best man, Bob, raised his glass to his "Brother Carolyn," oops! We all broke out in laughter at that one as wedding-day jitters washed away with the champagne. Rather than "Muskrat Love," we settled on "Everything I Do, I Do It for You," as sung by Bryan

Adams. The lyrics of that song had always resonated with me, and I often imagined them as a love song between Christ and His followers. I can be particularly emotional in my approach to God and try to bring those feelings into all areas of my life. It was fitting, then, that we use a melody that carried such overtones of spirituality as we celebrated our commitment to one another. We danced and my spirit sailed.

The time-honored traditions of throwing the garter and bouquet were interesting. Peter caught the garter and the panties Tom had up his sleeve that he pretended to remove from me. He wore each around his arm, and said that he felt like a general. He didn't realize that catching them meant he was next in line for the altar, and he claims to have gone into a state of panic when he learned what the custom signified. Rachel was in perfect form when she made a long reach to catch my bouquet and was married less than a year later. We're still waiting for Peter.

We ate, danced, and enjoyed friends and relatives for hours. Finally, we made our getaway to the honeymoon suite. A huge room, including wet bar and hot tub, were waiting for our tired, but elated bodies. Initially I felt disappointed that we were unable to have an afternoon wedding, with ours at 11:00 in the morning. My opinion changed now that we had an evening still stretched before us to luxuriously enjoy. We left the reception at 7:00; it had been a long and wonderful day.

After a long soak and sweet time alone, we drifted off to sleep in the king-sized waterbed. When I awoke, it was thundering and lightening outside, and rain was drenching the city. I thought how lucky we were to have sunny skies early in the day. It was late in the evening, and as Tom slept I lay there in contemplation, considering the new life I faced now joined in marriage to this man.

Would we pool our strengths the way I had envisioned,

to become more than just the sum of our parts? Had something mystical already begun to work a change in us? I only felt contentment and happiness at this moment. My impatience could use the influence of his well-composed temperament, and perhaps my organizational ability would take the edge from his sometimes scattered responsibilities.

A poetic reading given by Cayce expresses my thinking on this matter: "These as individuals chose one another as companions. For what? Because they fitted into such companionship, becoming more and more daily as one and as a complement as one, finding in the other that which would answer their needs . . . Let each be the complement, the mortise and pestle, or the dew upon the flower, or the rainbow in the cloud, or as the voices in the night." (2072-15)

My husband began to stir and brought me back to the moment at hand. There would be time for reflection later; now was the time for being about the business of living the first day of our new life together!

# 14

# Beginnings

> "The gem cannot be polished without friction, nor man perfected without trials."
> —Chinese Proverb

HUGH Lynn Cayce, the late son of Edgar Cayce, once posed the engaging question in an A.R.E. lecture he gave: "Whom are you creating?" The thrust of his speech centered on the attitudes that we form, nourish, and carry with us that make us who we are. He emphasized that we are actually creating the person we will be twenty years or twenty lifetimes from now (let's hope it doesn't take that long to "get it").

Just as true is the knowledge that a marriage between two people is a creation in progress. An atmosphere is built around them, either of love, indifference, or hate. It is formed by the actions they choose that say, "I respect you; I value your presence in my life." Or, "My own comfort and happiness comes before yours, get outa my way!" It's not easy. Most of us have a variety of issues to work through, and in a marriage relationship they are intensified and impossible to ignore. I am realizing that more and more, as I walk the path of partnership that began when I said "I do."

Learning to react with kindness instead of criticism takes time for some of us. The decision to place our fears and worries in the hands of God is a repetitive one. The spiritual muscles lose strength if not consciously exercised, and it's easy to become flabby from indifference. These are areas in which I am continuously presented with opportunities in my marriage for developing positive attitudes so that if I'm ever asked that loaded question, "Whom are you creating?!" I won't have to stutter and duck away.

I often find myself relearning what I thought I already knew. Impatience has gripped my throat so tightly at times that it's difficult for myself and everyone in my proximity to breathe. How I'd love to be blessed with an almost always even temper, a real joy to be around twenty-four hours a day. Ha! I can't wish my shortcomings away, but I can begin the hard job of building a character that is more in line with my ideal. It's easy to slip into old habits and ways of reacting—oh, to never again be a bitch!—so I'm trying to keep a check on my frame of mind.

Unfortunately, it is my husband who most often bears the brunt of my growing pains. Blame it on hormonal curse if you like, but the moods sometimes swing. I don't like it when my personality darkens the air around me and my nastiness is set off by something as unbearable as having to wait.

I am usually on time or a few minutes early for everything, a trait I inherited from my parents. When they pick me up at airports, I know I will find them seated right inside the gate as I deplane. My husband, on the other hand, would send me reeling from shock if he ever stepped foot in the airport before my bags were making their third trip around the carousel. It's just his nature to get there in the nick of time, and it makes me a nervous wreck.

When preparing for our first party after we were married, I asked him to pick up the ice for the cooler along with the drinks. He left early in the afternoon as I commenced to clean house and prepare food. I scrubbed the kitchen floor, vacuumed, and worked on meatballs and dips, and still he hadn't returned. Hours had clicked by when, finally, he came through the door. I looked on incredulously as he brought in bag after bag of an odd assortment of party favors and lights, but no ice or drinks. We were an hour away from the first guest arriving, and neither of us had showered, yet he was beginning to undertake hanging lights from our back porch. I could feel the anger in my chest spreading and building until it erupted in hot tears and choked-out words of fury.

The disappointment and rage colored my mind for quite awhile before finally ebbing away. But I knew that I was missing the boat somehow; getting mad never solves the problem—it usually makes it worse. Especially when trying to force others to be something they're not. Later, I would ask myself why I couldn't have simply been delighted that Tom had the creative urge to make the party more festive? As it turned out, he purchased the ice and drinks and was ready when the doorbell began to ring. I had wasted energy and contributed to negative patterns that I knew I didn't want in my life. Still, the anger was real, and I couldn't have just wished it away. There had to be another way.

A fresh occasion for choosing a different reaction came at Christmas time. We were invited to a string of elegant holiday parties. When the night of the first one arrived, I felt anxious about arriving for them on time. Tom had gone to the office to complete some paperwork and still hadn't returned home. I was trying not to become tense, but the waiting and staring at the clock was slowly getting to me. I decided to relax in a bath while I waited. I filled the tub with hot, bubbling water and brought candles into the room. I turned out the lights, leaving a soft flickering glow to dance on the walls around me. Ahhh . . . it felt great to warm my muscles, sore from a workout earlier in the day. The scent from the waxed vanilla completed the luxurious atmosphere.

As I slipped deeper into the soothing water, I began a prayer that went something like this: "Lord, You know how I feel about being on time. You know me better than anyone, and You're aware of how upset I can get. Please help me to let go of the desire to control this area of my life, so that I can just enjoy the evening with Tom. Be the intercessor between us so that he is reminded of my feelings without my having to say anything. Communicate between our spirits to bring understanding. Thank You for helping me release this. Amen."

I lay there soaking for several minutes when I heard the key turn in the lock. He was later than he'd predicted, but not horribly so. His jaw was unmoving, as if to brace himself for my impatience. Instead, I gave him a huge, wet hug and a big smile. He looked at me suspiciously, as though waiting for the other shoe to drop. It didn't, I'm happy to say, and we dressed unhurriedly and arrived just as his partner did. Everything went much more smoothly when I didn't push and shove, and we had a great time at the party. Thanks, Lord.

It's taken me a while to learn that I have neither the right nor the ability to change anyone else. I do have a responsibility to alter my own thoughts and attitudes, however, and it's worth the effort when I consider the long-term implications. At any time we choose, we may experience peace instead of conflict within our minds rather than reacting in the familiar knee-jerk patterns.

In relationships between men and women, particularly when the two are married, there is the tendency to take one another for granted. I have had a few moments when I seemed to leave my cloudy state of thinking and see the root of this problem very clearly.

We often begin to sense other persons as simply an extension of ourselves, literally. When we're rude as we would never be with a co-worker or friend, I believe it's because we're not only disrespecting our mate, but essentially ourselves. I am not denying the oneness of all God's creation, but even in unity we are still individuals, worthy of respect. It can be easy to forget that and take out our disappointments with ourselves on others. Parents sometimes do this with children, when they become caught up in wanting to make good impressions on others to the detriment of the child. I've done this with Tom. I have been upset with him in a very negative way and lost sight of the knowledge that he is entitled to make his own mistakes and be exactly who he is regardless of whether it fits my image of him or not.

One night quite late I experienced the lifting of this veil in a quite extraordinary way. The two of us had worked past midnight at the office, attending to the never-ending stream of paperwork that he is inundated by. We arrived home, watched the end of a bad movie on television, and it was after 2:00 a.m. when I looked up at him standing beside my chair. I hadn't been thinking any particularly mystical thoughts or anything; I felt exhausted, when suddenly I became covered with goose bumps. He stood there talking, and it was as if I were seeing him for the first time. I felt almost embarrassed by my casual manner and look, there in my wrinkled blue nightgown, hair all afluff. I thought, I really admire this man, and I don't let him know it often enough. I criticize more than compliment him, and just look at how amazing he is.

It's as though I'd glimpsed the real person, and the blasé

attitude that begins to form at times disappeared. It was helpful because now I can recall that experience whenever I start to take him for granted. It reminded me of a dream I had had the night before:

> Imprisoned with a group of people, I am trying to escape. My parents are helping me, and one of my strongest thoughts and feelings concerns Tom. I am afraid that I won't see him again and that I have not let him know how much I love him. My actions had sometimes shown impatience and moodiness. I longed to change that.

What I've come to realize and am continually being reminded is that love really is a choice, not a surge of rushing emotion. Personalities may clash, and when they do the choice is available to build a bridge of peace, rather than a fortress of pain. Cayce had this to say about the marriage relationship: "Then when ye are, either of thee in turmoil—*not* one shall do *all* the praying, nor all the 'cussing'; but *together—ask!* and He will give—as He has promised—that assurance of peace, of harmony, that can *only* come from a coordinated, cooperative effort on the part of souls that seek to be the channels through which His love, His glory may be manifested in the earth!" (1523-6)

To be a part of a team that works together, struggling sometimes to put into practice the spiritual ideals that are deeply felt in the calm—and difficult to express in the storm—is part of the beauty of married life. I have seen the effects that cooperation may bring: laughter, consideration of feelings, respect for the other's wishes. In stark contrast are the effects of consternation allowed to rule: harsh words, raised voices, mean acts of revenge. One brings peace, the other a household war.

When there is an obvious difference in opinion about a

domestic matter, there can be continuously ruffled feathers if it isn't worked out fairly. In our case this often manifests as Pack Rat vs. White Tornado, I being the latter. I have moved often enough that I've developed a strong distaste for piles of belongings that are never used. I clear out my closets frequently, and if more than a year has gone by without my wearing something, to the Goodwill truck it goes. I prefer to eliminate as much unnecessary clutter as possible. My partner, on the other hand, believes there will always be a use for items somewhere down the line.

We joke about the time he wanted to hang onto an old, ripped-up shirt. His argument was that it could be put on the end of a handle and used as a dust mop! Now whenever there is a disagreement about the worth of something hanging around our house, I tease him with, "Yes, we could put it on the end of a handle and mop the floor," and he laughs through clenched teeth. It's really sticky at times, and a sense of humor is the only weapon that can break the tension without resorting to bodily harm.

Just this morning we had a bit of a row, as the British say, over a soap tin he brought back from our anniversary stay in a fancy hotel. I had thrown it in the bathroom garbage since I had already put away four others, as well as five shower caps and a bag full of the little shampoos that the hotel provides. Since this stray one was left out, I simply disposed of it. He took it out of the garbage and let me know that he's saving it to put thumb tacks in. I got miffed since I had already found a home in our cramped apartment for all the other items, and didn't like being reprimanded for one extra soap tin. Recycling was far from my mind at the moment.

I got a little ugly about it and told him I'd have to throw other items out to make room for it. Them's fightin' words to an avid preserver of "stuff," and I knew it. We played a quick round of verbal jarts (they're bigger than darts), and he left for work less than serene. I moped around for a while, feeling justified in my anger. After all, I'm the one who has to clean this place and find somewhere to store our many piles of journals, paperwork, and such (a case of poor me in action). The more I thought about it, though, the more ridiculous it became, until it dawned on me that I was doing exactly what I had vowed to myself I'd try not to do and that was attack him for something that is such a part of him.

What now? I knew I couldn't simply expect my strong feelings about the subject to just fall away, so there would have to be another method of dealing with this recurrent problem. What did the reading say? Together, ask. That's what we would need to do in order to restore harmony. I called him during the lunch hour to do just that.

My husband is, fortunately for me, very quick to forgive harsh words and start over again without grudges. His response when I called to utter a prayer? "Aren't we silly arguing over such petty stuff? We need to find something more worthy than a 2-by-4 soap tin to fight about!" He always puts things in perspective, but I know that it is most often those seemingly trivial things that can drive a marriage to the divorce court. We can't let them accumulate and wear away at our relationship, and with God directing us we have the ultimate odds in our favor.

It isn't always a struggle, although the negative challenges seem to get the most attention. When we manage to strike the right chords and get into a groove that works, being together can be remarkable. I've learned not to take for granted the moments of cooperation that can produce miracles when allowed to.

Creating a home full of the good vibrations that love and respect bring is the challenge we are trying to meet. The vows we made were only the beginning of a day-by-day reaffirming of whom we serve and how we choose to treat one another. Simply saying "I do" does not an inseparable bond create. What it does is weave together the tie that is either strengthened or unraveled over time. Whom are we creating? With the help of the Holy Spirit, a home that breathes life to all who visit and says in a loud whisper that "Love lives here"!

## 15

# *From the Mouths of Babes*

> "The great man is he who does not lose his child's heart."
> —Mencius

MY greatest teachers have usually been well below the legal voting age. Kids possess qualities that oftentimes atrophy in many of us as we "mature" and become immersed in the daily routine of living and surviving. When things get complicated in my grown-up world, their curiosity, honesty, and depth of trust remind me of the excitement felt when first uncovering the mysteries of life. If I listen closely and try to resist the urge to interpret everything for them from my own limited view, their influence resurrects my long-forgotten powers of imagination and ability to believe the sometimes unbelievable. Life truly became sweeter when my four nephews entered and presented me with whole new worlds of possibility.

This all-encompassing curiosity that they bring to almost every situation has often forced me to think and rethink my attitudes about areas of concern that I thought I had already worked out in my mind. They've taught me that seldom are issues as cut and dry as they seem when held to the light of inquisitive innocence.

One of my little guys, Jeff, asked when he was about two years old, "Aunt Carolyn, who's the debil (devil)?" We had been sitting in the afternoon sun reading Bible stories together from the children's Bible that he loved. With those big brown eyes looking expectantly into mine, I knew I couldn't walk around this one. His simple question hung in the air as I collected my thoughts. My boy wanted to know, and I needed to be as simple and straightforward as I could be.

I searched my brain for the information—it had to be there somewhere. It was not as neatly tucked away as I'd have liked. How could this be?! I had read and studied Bible verses, as well as the Cayce files on evil, but any concrete definition they might have helped me to form about our man Satan was suddenly a blank in my memory bank. I feel that many of the Bible stories are symbolic of deeper truths, but I couldn't say with certainty that this was one of them. And how does a two year old comprehend symbolism? Various interpretations clouded my mind in contradictory competition.

With a quick prayer for help, I heard myself saying, "You know, I don't know everything about the devil, but I know who God is. God loves you like Daddy and Mommy and I love you. If you talk to Him and to Jesus when you need help, He'll be right here with you. Jesus said that you don't need to be afraid because He is always with you. The devil tempted Jesus with all the power and money in the world if He would give up on the work God had given Him to do. He told him that He wasn't interested, and there was nothing that the devil could do to make Him change His mind. We don't need to be afraid of the devil, because Jesus proved that He is stronger than him any day." He smiled and nodded his head in agreement and echoed with a look of awe the title of a little book I'd given him, "Jesus knows me!"

Afterward, I struggled to crystallize my shaky knowledge—for myself and for Jeff, because I knew from experience how confusing the conflicting messages we hear can be. I read the words of Jesus more closely, searching for His teaching on who "the devil" is. What I saw clearly is that while Jesus speaks of a devil, He puts ultimate emphasis on His own saving power. So whether we choose to think of Satan as a spirit of evil trying constantly to lead us astray or as the spirit of rebellion within all of us or even as both, the over and over again message that Christ taught was that we have nothing to fear! Years later, I found it expressed beautifully by Herbert Bruce Puryear in his book *Why Jesus Taught Reincarnation:*

> It is not a question of whether there is a devil. The question is to what position of power is he to be elevated in our thoughts? The Bible makes it clear that he is clearly subservient to God. The Bible is not dualistic as many Christians believe. It is not a battle of the forces of light against the forces of darkness, as though God is impotent in the face of the devil.
>
> So how does the devil get to be so powerful? He does so just as a Hitler or a Mafia boss, by recruiting like-minded lieutenants and playing upon the negative emotions and desires, especially after the lust for power. After all, that is the best he had to offer Jesus. (p. 210)

Reading Puryear's book was a great relief in looking back

at my conversation with two-year-old Jeff, who was by then ten. The questioning mind and heart of a child is handed to us with a great responsibility attached. It's important, I have found, to admit to myself that I don't have all the answers, but I do know where to look.

Very early Jeff showed a deep interest in the life of Jesus. More than that, he has the attitude that says he has taken to heart the command to love, as his gentle concern for the feelings of others often demonstrates. I believe that we each have a distinct calling in our lives, and it's fascinating to watch these four boys develop into theirs. How crucial it is to not be too quick to dismiss them with pat answers. The natural trust with which they ask reminds me that I still have much to learn and have a grand privilege in sharing my piece of the truth.

It's true that children sometimes lie when faced with an accusatory finger, as most humans have at some time in their lives. This aside, I have marveled at the more basic instinct to reveal themselves in an honest, no-holds-barred fashion. It's sad that we adults often lose so much of this ability as we age. If they're angry, you know it. There is seldom the need to figure out what toddlers are thinking. They will make you clearly aware. So often as grownups we sit wondering if someone else is upset with us and why. The instant feedback given by a four year old is refreshing as well as jolting in its unrefined expression, but it brings to me the realization that I need to be more up-front in my own relationships. Resentments allowed to grow and fester have created too many ulcers and cancers in our world already.

The oldest of my four, Greg, had a creative method for airing his opinions without being overtly offensive: through the voice of his imaginary friend, Elliot. Many years have passed since our family was entertained by the Adventures of Elliot. There was a time, however, when this invisible boy went everywhere my nephew did, and he seemed to have done everything and know just about all things as well.

If he needed to disagree or express distaste, Elliot was available to help out. When there was a question about what to have for dinner, Elliot's preferences were always considered. "Elliot doesn't like gravy. Elliot likes butter on his potatoes." That settled that! Butter it would be. His pal allowed him at age four or five to begin to assert a different opinion in a somewhat safe way.

Coaxing Greg to ignore a suggestion of Elliot's in favor of family plans was difficult, but could be done. Once when driving him the thirty miles to visit his great-grandma Marsh, my mom found herself having to present a case in favor of the trip to Elliot via Greg, since it seems the invisible friend wanted to stay at home and play. When reassured that a swing set would be waiting in the yard, Elliot voiced his approval from the back seat! After that he loved visiting Grandma Marsh, especially when he discovered her remarkable cooking skills and loving ways.

Being the oldest had presented Greg with special needs, and creatively he met the task of disagreeing and being heard with the artful help of his playmate. He is to this day a tactful young man who will find a way to make his needs known without bulldozing over others. In Elliot he had a comrade who was quite experienced (he was a doctor, had lived in the woods, and knew people such as television's Mr. Rogers personally, among many other things) and able to speak up for what he wanted. Thanks, Elliot, for brightening all our lives, especially one little boy who was finding his own voice through you.

While I know that I can't conjure an imaginary playmate of my own without risk of friends questioning my sanity, what I realize in considering Elliot's purpose is that all of us would do well to consider ourselves our own secret friend. Sometimes we are most unkind to ourselves, and it helps to step aside and see that we're deserving of the little acts of compassion that help lighten the way.

Two boys each were born to my two older brothers, and the younger two—Tim and Jason—came in a two-year succession. Much research exists concerning birth order and its effect on personality. I know from my experience with these four that the youngest in each family, like me, are a bit more rebellious in spirit. Maybe it's because we feel the need to make our strengths known or maybe we're just the "babies" competing for attention. Whatever the reason, it is interesting to watch the drama unfold. While we youngest born can create a ruckus, we also have a great ability to display trust. We tend to look up to our older counterparts with great admiration when we're not crying that they get to do everything we can't do. We were lucky enough to have someone before us breaking new ground, and it really secretly delights us to have the parental hold loosened just a bit by the time we arrive.

The nephews who each hold the title of youngest in my brothers' families began very early to display the worshipful trust that little brothers often have for their older siblings. In one situation, we all watched as Greg became the "spokesman" for his baby brother, Tim. They seemed to have their own wordless language that enabled the oldest to often interpret for the rest of us what the other needed. In fact, this arrangement worked so well that in view of the help he was getting, he decided to put off learning to speak for a while, relying on the help of his older brother to relay his wishes.

The one born last into our family, Jason, also looked to his big brother for the crowning touch of agreement on many things. I would smile inside each time he would make an authoritative statement and then look up and say to his brother, "Right, Jeff?" Such love and trust in between the wrestling and fighting.

I had a wider space of years between my brothers and

me than these two, but I had many of the same feelings of admiration. I remember thinking that my brothers were the coolest guys alive, and I fantasized that I would join in on their pranks and fun away from home. Being nearly seven and eight years older than I, though, it was not to be until I was much older. I shed many angry tears at not being able to go where they went and do what they did.

Once, on an annual picnic that our family shared with several others, I was feeling left out when my brothers, Mike and Jim, started off on a walk with some of the teen-age girls who were daughters of a friend of our family. They were holding hands and laughing. My ten-year-old hand decided to grab the same of an eight year old and take him walking with me. The little boy wasn't thrilled, letting out a loud "Oooh, gross!" as he wrenched his hand from mine, and I resigned myself to playing on the swings instead. But oh, how I secretly wished I could be included in my big brothers' adventures.

Perhaps one reason Jesus emphasizes the fact that He is our "elder brother" is because this relationship has such great potential. With a brother or sister we're not alone, and there doesn't necessarily have to be a blood tie in order to have that connection. We have someone to love and emulate with great affection. We know that He will do battle for us when the situation arises, will teach us what He has already learned.

In ideal circumstances, family represents safety and love, unconditionally. We learn the most basic lessons within our family, and we develop the ability to get along with others. Edgar Cayce suggested that family life presents the greatest opportunities for soul growth. After all, Jesus' only command was that we love one another. What better occasion to begin to learn what that means than in the everyday life of a family, with all the clashes of personality and struggle for identity, as well as the long-remembered fun and play.

It's not so much a matter of memorizing the Golden Rule in hopes of earning a gold star in Sunday school, although learning it is important; but it's how we handle the fact that there's only one toy available and two sets of hands to share it. Or learning to have patience as a little sister who has to sometimes stay behind.

With our "elder brother" we, too, can stand up for what we believe, then look to Him and ask, "Right, Jesus?"—ready to be helped and corrected if we're off base. He also taught us that God our Father is to be called "Abba," meaning "Daddy." I think we can begin to see how our spiritual life is meant to be a family experience, not a thing far removed from everyday life.

That spirit of love and family connection that Jesus tries to communicate to us is the supreme law that encompasses all others. How lucky I feel to have Him as close as a prayer, available to me and mine always. When my youngest brother was divorced and his two boys moved from their home, Jesus helped pave the way for healing and happiness in the midst of a situation that was difficult for everyone.

As has been true many times in my life, I feel that I was led to be home in Decatur during this rocky period. I have moved around frequently, but often find myself back in the heartland for stretches of time. I had been home a year when my brother and his wife divorced. It was quick, not bitter or drawn out, which was fortunate. The whirlwind of events meant that two of my nephews would be adjusting to a new home and set of circumstances. They are two incredibly resilient kids and found ways to make the transition less difficult for themselves. Still, it was not easy for them. One worry that was apparent in their young minds was that their daddy would not have companionship now that they could not be there all the time. One encouraged me to move in with him, into their old bedroom. Nothing could touch my heart more than the unselfish caring of a three year old for his dad. They soon felt comfortable with my being just a short walk away, and they could relax a bit knowing that their father had a place to eat his dinners and sit and talk if he wanted to.

When the time had come for the new school year to start, they faced another trial. Jeff would be entering first grade in a different school. When the big day arrived, his mom walked him to the bus stop, lending her support to his trembling heart. Unfortunately, it was not the correct bus, and he found himself at the wrong school. That experience may have colored his attitude toward the new school irreparably, because he continued to be filled with fear about the prospect of having to continue there even after finding the right classroom.

One evening at a local pizza parlor, his fear came tumbling out in tears and pleas to not have to return there or have his little brother Jason attend kindergarten there the following year. I could see that my brother didn't know what to do at this point, so later when I was alone with my nephews the three of us looked to our Helper for some resolution. We pulled to the side of the road and the three of us joined hands. I prayed, "Lord, please take over here. If it's Your will that they be in this school, then help bring relief to the fear that we are experiencing; if not, then take him out of there, please!" Jeff's first response was to resist the possibility that it could be God's will for him to be there, and he cried out, "No! I don't want to go to school there!" But I reassured him that Jesus would take care of him and bring his suffering to an end one way or another. My heart was breaking, but I really believed that our prayer would move whatever mountains stood in the way of his adjustment.

It wasn't long after this that his mom and dad decided to put him back into the school he had attended the year before near his old home, and since they have joint custody, this was a feasible solution. Thank You, heavenly Father, for giving me the gift of two little boys to help me learn the power of prayer and faith, and thank You for letting me share in their joy and relief when You intervene.

Three weeks before my wedding all but the oldest of the four came to spend the night with me. We have always enjoyed spending lots of our time together: picnics in the park, long walks, hikes (where we sometimes had trouble finding our way out of the trails), movies, and McDonald's. This was our last great hurrah before I'd be leaving them for a while. We had a great time! The lawn sprinkler in the afternoon, with Jason, the youngest of them all, getting annoyed at the older two and their disrespect for his attempts at nailing down the plastic sliding sheet. I caught his look of exasperation on film, as Jeff and Tim went sailing down before Jason could complete the task at hand. Our little celebration was perfect: the mall in the evening with a Hardee's late lunch, several rented movies, pizza, our traditional bedtime stories in which I made them the central characters, and my poor decision to put all three in one bed. Midway through the night I was creating beds on the floor. The next morning I cooked all of their favorites, and Jason remarked that his pancake was shaped like Florida. The mention of my soon-to-be new home state made me painfully aware of the bridge we were drawing close together. Oh, how I would miss them! My heart ached already.

The smiles they bring me are worth every tear, and the lessons they remind me of can be hilarious. While spending a week with me after my marriage, Jason was trying to show everyone his authority by continually telling us to "shut up"! Jeff was getting aggravated and tried to figure out ways to get him to stop with the loud commands. We had spent a day at Sea World, and on the trip back home I let them talk on the CB radio. Jason was trying to get someone to speak to him and asked several times, "Does anyone out there care to chat?" (I had coached him on what to say.) Suddenly, over the radio came the booming voice of a trucker, "No one wants to talk, so would you just SHUT UP!"

Jason looked stunned, then we all burst out laughing, and I informed him that he had just experienced a great law of the universe—what goes around, comes around! His "shut ups" became less frequent for a while.

When I am with them, my world stretches a bit beyond its usual boundaries. I always thought that the flowery statements on greeting cards that assure us that miles cannot really separate us were just sentimental wishful thinking. In a sense they are. After all, now that I'm away, I can't pick them up from school as I've done so many times and whisk them to the duck pond or the toy section of my favorite religious bookstore. That hurts. Sweet words that try to diminish that pain only serve to stuff it down until it demands release. No, physical separation cannot be metaphysically swept away, not entirely at least. But I also know that there is no separation when love is the connection. Still, I look forward to Christmas family visits and summertime stays.

I feel that the day is fast approaching, after the hard days are over, when Jesus will walk this earth again with us. I am assured of that in my Bible, by the Edgar Cayce readings, through the messages of Mary, and as the still, small voice in my heart speaks to me. When that day comes, I know that all those I love will be able to share in my joy as we walk a different walk with the Master. Somehow when I see my boys, I know it even more fully. Then the illusion of our being apart will truly crumble into dust.

My nephews are four of the greatest blessings that have ever been given to me. Through them I see myself with more caring eyes. They are teachers who show me what love really is. They're not tiny any more; they are fast becoming young men. Watching them grow and being a part of the process has been quite a trip, and I know that the best is yet to be!

## 16

## *Awaiting the Gift*

> "When we have done our best, we should wait the result in peace." —Author Unknown

BECOMING a parent is one of the scariest and most beautiful experiences I have to look forward to. My four nephews have helped me realize the joy it can bring. When I began to contemplate the possibility of being a mom, I made some unexpected discoveries about myself and my faith in the God of adventure whom I follow. I will wind down that road again, back to the day that helped stir a longing deep within.

A soft rain was falling as we drove through the side streets of St. Augustine, the oldest city in the United States—full of the visions of many yesterdays. With a day of browsing through the many unique shops and restaurants finished, my mom and I were making our way back to Jacksonville. My mind wasn't on babies; it was driven by my stomach's desire to get back quickly and make dinner for my husband and parents who were spending a November vacation in our home. The sign pointing to the shrine of Our Lady of La Leche changed my plans, and I turned the car around. My hunger pangs could wait while my mom and I explored the place that held such a touch of mystery for me.

We quickly parked and made our way across the grounds, noting statues of Mary, St. Francis, and a cross marking the site where the earliest American church was established. As we walked, I explained to my mother the story that had fascinated me.

Thirty-five years earlier, after several years of marriage and attempts to conceive a child, my mother-in-law had come to this very spot to pray. She and Tom's father were in St. Augustine on business, and while there she couldn't help but hope that this special place of prayer for mothers would aid her somehow. It was that week that she did indeed become the temporary home for a special soul—my husband, Tom.

He and I didn't learn of this until after he chose Florida as the place he wanted to live, a mere thirty miles from where she had prayed! I joke with them and note that he probably thought his home would be in St. Augustine and had a cold awakening nine months later when he was born at the end of January in New York. He spent the next thirty-three winters grumbling about the ice and snow and lamenting the fact that he needs sun.

Now, here I was, so many years later, kneeling in the same room as my mother-in-law had. Candles flickered at my side as I stared at the image of Mary. Her eyes seemed to hold a promise, seemed to speak to me of unknown tomorrows and long-forgotten yesterdays. And I prayed. Prayed for that grand commission of becoming a mom.

The mist covered us as we left the altar and moved on. I felt such lightness in my soul that I wanted to let everyone in on my secret. I'd been touched by the power of a thousand prayers in this place, held in the silence of Love. I knew that the time to prepare myself had arrived. I remembered the words from a reading that had excited me many years earlier: "Too oft individuals are too prone to look upon conception or childbirth as purely a physical condition. Rather should it be considered, as it has been from the beginning, that life—sources of life—is from the one source... Remember how Hannah prepared herself, and as to how others—as Mary—prepared themselves. There are many [such cases] recorded, and there are many others of which nothing is heard, and yet there was the long preparation." (2977-2)

The Bible tells us that the life within Elizabeth leaped and caused her to prophesy the words that would become the cornerstone of the faithful, "Blessed art thou among women, and blessed is the fruit of thy womb" (Luke 1:42), upon hearing Mary's greeting. The two women spent three months together, Mary at the beginning of her pregnancy, Elizabeth nearing the end of hers. What sorts of preparation did they participate in?

The readings pointed me toward an unfolding understanding. Since I accept that the nature of the soul is eternal, spanning time both before birth and after death, I know that what grows within the body when a man and woman combine is a vessel for a soul to come again into the earth to learn and continue to grow spiritually. This means that the thoughts before and during conception have an effect, as well as the attitudes held throughout the pregnancy, on the type of human being attracted. Anger, hatred, self-condemnation—all these carry a vibration that can be perceived by that soul.

At home after my St. Augustine experience, I shared my vision with Tom. There was a glint in his eyes—was it excitement? Or apprehension? Perhaps a bit of both. My trip to La Leche was the catalyst that stirred whatever parental yearnings we already felt inside.

Discussions opened. The prospect of having a little person to guide, teach, and love took center stage in our conversations. The need for both of us to be as physically sound as we are able was in the forefront of my doctor-husband's mind. My strong desire to be centered spiritually dominated mine. Our task was before us; it was ours to carry it out.

I was aware of the way my mental attitude changes according to my surroundings. Friends have often heard me comment rather theatrically that if God needed to punish me He would only have to place me in a dark underground nightclub with no windows, filled with cigarette smoke and bad music (usually I am in such a place just described when I am moved to make such a declaration). Consciously, I determined to try to eliminate such downers as much as possible. Music, movies, books, food, hugs, and warm baths all have the potential for creating good vibrations instead.

I began looking for sounds that help me feel centered, not scattered. I dusted off my classical guitar and began picking out some love songs with my Willie Nelson and James Taylor CDs. Though my playing was hit and miss when it came to choosing the right notes, the guitar made such a beautiful sound that it all rather blended together anyway (at least to my ears).

My love of music is familial. My father is a very good guitarist and singer and can play almost any instrument by ear. He serenaded us with Merle Haggard and Johnny Cash songs for many years. His father and uncle were semiprofessional musicians, playing in the taverns around rural Illinois. Maintaining a happy, positive frame of mind is much easier when done to a backdrop of good tunes.

Give me Haydn and a thick book, and I achieve a state of

near bliss. As a little girl, I escaped into the written word as much as possible, and it was like living a secret life within the pages of each book. Any piece of work done by artists in touch with their center is a help to the mind and spirit, whether or not the authors mention the name of God. Truly spirit-infused work is simply the result of really reaching inside for the essence, and doing it well.

I began to see that when I honor the movement of creation that is all around me, I honor the Supreme Creator. In contemplating the offering of my body for another person and truly co-creating with God, I recognized how far I strayed from that realization at times and how all important it is to vigilantly prevent that from happening. I was beginning to find cause for celebrating life everywhere.

Ah, the benefits of the sensuality of touch. We all know what happened to the little ones who were left in their cribs devoid of human caressing and holding (what a ghastly way to prove a point!); they failed to "thrive," to progress as they should in development. Getting enough hugs is always important, but I've also found other ways of getting my tactile needs met.

I love water. Hot, bubbly water to soak and relax in. Recognizing that when one is actually pregnant, water temperatures have to be closely monitored to prevent damage to the fetus, I nixed hot tubs and headed for the bath tub. Stimulating the sensitive nerve endings in the skin with silky, warm water is a religious experience. The baby is going to get nine months of this wonderment, so Momma may as well have some, too.

It's amazing how merely setting the wheels in motion to prepare myself mentally for conception and pregnancy caused me to become so much more aware, with even the choice of a television program laden with potential! Mental gestation was only one corner of the triangle, though. Physical training had to take its place as well. Along with feeding my mind through music and books, I began scrutinizing my culinary habits as well.

I've always had a preference for a diet with minimal meat. I remember my mom getting aggravated when I would eat the crust from her delicious fried chicken and leave the rest. She would look at me with motherly eyes and say, "Carolyn Sue, just look at all the meat that's left on that bone!" Sorry, Mom. Once after eating at a friend's house, her mother called to ask my mom if there was anything wrong with her spaghetti; it seems I had carefully piled all the hamburger to one side and ate only the noodles and sauce. My poor mother met a challenge when she had me.

I am more and more convinced that the value of animal food has decreased drastically over the last twenty years. The chickens that once ran free now live caged in tight quarters awaiting their slaughter, being pumped with antibiotics and hormones in the meantime. I find it much more fun to seek out exotic vegetables and fruits to experiment with—and far more healthy. However, even the green and yellow fellows have their drawbacks in this twentieth century we're in.

Harmful pesticides cling to our vegetables and fruits. A friend suggested soaking them in water, lemon juice, and salt to remove the unwanted chemicals, and that is what I have been doing. I don't know how thoroughly this gets the job done, but I'm sure it helps. The other alternative is to either grow them myself, which I have done with some success in the past, or buy them from a farm that produces organically. Because our soil has changed since the pioneer days, even organic foods might be lacking in essential nutrients. That is why my nutrition-conscious husband approaches me with a multivitamin each morning. It's his way of saying I love you!

All of this talk about proper diet and so forth might sound restrictive, and I don't mean it to. I am very lenient with myself. If I crave something, I usually go for it. I have simply outlined for myself the desires that I have for emphasizing what I've learned so that I can be the best me possible when I'm home for another person. We do our best, that is all that's required. What is right for me might not be right for someone else; each body is different, and God is always waiting for us to tune in and find out what He would have us do in our period of preparation.

The most important influence, of course, is Tom's and my prayers and desires. The longing for God's will, not ours, to be done through the acts of conception, pregnancy, and birth. I continue to be shown that our most wonderful, amazing fantasies for ourselves pale in comparison to the will of God and what He would do through us. My own individual intentions suddenly began to be cloudy when I wrote them on paper. Clarifying my desires for my child helped me uncover some hidden errors in my thinking.

When I put ink to paper and stated that I wanted to be open to God's will entirely, by not dictating through my own wishes what this baby will be like, I started to write the word "except . . . " and had planned to follow that with "that the child be spiritually inclined," when I stopped and drew a line through "except." I realized that if I included that last line, I wasn't really open to God's will at all. For, it is possible that His will could include sending a child who needs desperately to learn, who hasn't "advanced" as much as I would have liked for him or her. Perhaps if I'm open to whatever God would have me do, I will be challenged by someone in need of basic lessons in the loving department. It's a scary thought. Do I trust God enough to take that chance?

Then another thought came. Almost every expectant mother, when asked what she is hoping for, responds, "A healthy baby." If I'm laying even that basic desire on the altar, so to speak, then I must be ready for the possibility of a less than physically perfect child with the blessings and opportunities they can bring. I'm certainly not saying that God delights in "giving it to us" when we've agreed to accept His will. His law is perfect Love, and I know that firsthand. It's just that not every lesson is learned without difficulty and to say, "Here am I, send me, use me," carries the exhilaration of the baby bird's first tumble from the safe warm nest, simultaneously thrilling, yet dangerously unknown.

Another more obvious scenario that I had considered but not dwelled upon was the possibility that motherhood might not be one of my roles to fill this time around.

All of the potential mars in my perfect picture are not punishments by a hateful God; rather, they are lessons agreed upon by each soul involved either for the purpose of instruction and learning or as fulfillment of a law. They are entered into in cooperation with God in the spirit of love, not out of fear or self-condemnation. I had to be ready to walk the walk of faith whether or not a cradle is filled.

These ideas needed to be addressed, then released. I had made an important realization about surrender, and now I could move on because I know that I know that Love's presence in my life will always take tender care of me. I will try my best to provide, whatever soul may come to me, a fit and worthy vessel by keeping body, mind, and spirit healthy. Beyond that, I would need to place the outcome in the keeping of the Holy Spirit.

The preparatory period before making babies lends a special sort of excitement to everyday living, and somewhere in the universe my St. Augustine prayer is still blending and moving with those of the mothers before me.

# 17

## Slaying Dragons

> "Be careful for nothing; but in every thing by prayer and supplication with thanksgiving let your requests be made known unto God."
> —Philippians 4:6

"WHY worry when you can pray?" is classic Cayce advice especially needed by career-worriers like me. My unconscious motto has probably gone more like, "Why not worry, just in case?" In case of what? Somehow I think that if I've already suffered the worst-case scenario in my mind, it won't hurt as badly when it actually happens. Yet I know that taking a fatalistic stance can help bring about the thing I fear most. Everyone knows a pessimist who seems to take pleasure in watching his or her dreaded predictions come to pass. Thoughts are things, the Cayce readings insist. They create our world.

Whether I'm Aunt Carolyn to my nephews, Mommy to future children, or Sweetie to my husband, I need to always try to be something more—a positive force—who knows from where her strength comes.

There is a lot of talk about "letting go and letting God," and undoubtedly it sounds ridiculously passive to some. Actually, it requires a great deal of activity to put things in His hands and leave them there.

First of all, an inner dialogue must be alive. Prayer is crucial with a minute-by-minute turning to God during particularly stressful times. It is constructive. It re-creates circumstances. It is all-powerful. Anxious dark imaginings can only prove harmful to the process of allowing God to intervene. It isn't enough to mumble words and then continue to fret afterward. This type of prayer must be deeply felt and permitted to take root in the heart and mind, then spread into the entire being.

Following conversation with God comes the time for listening. Intentional quiet is what meditation is all about. Because every day I face challenges and options that I'm not always prepared for or informed enough to make decisions about, the decisive voice must come from within. The time to begin this practice is not in the middle of the storm, but when the air is relatively calm. I discovered that the hard way.

Silencing voices that would deter me from the still, small one is more difficult than it sounds. Add to that an overwhelming concern clouding the mind, and it is doubly hard. Persistently practiced during the "good times," meditation builds the foundation for amazing strength when the crisis hits. I experienced this to be true when my R.N. training culminated in a tense period of close scrutinizing of my clinical skills.

After several years as a licensed practical nurse, busy moving around the country and taking classes wherever I went, my registered nursing license was finally well within reach. The final step in my education was an intense three-day clinical evaluation. There are testing centers throughout the country that work with the university I was attending, and I chose to go to California. It would be a nice place to relax for a few days once the exam was over, and I could stay with my cousin, Todd.

The idea of an evaluator staring closely as I gave nursing care was terrifying. The mostly Ph.D. nurses who do this job are not there in the capacity of instructor or helper; they are there to simply watch and determine if every element specified by the university is completed in the assigned areas of care. Entering into the exam, the student doesn't know what procedures are going to be required. It could be something as simple as listening to lung sounds or as complicated as administering pediatric intravenous medication in minute dosages. Those of us from all over the country gathered in the lobby of our hotel early Saturday morning, white faced and trembling. We had all heard horror stories of nurses failing because they forgot to wash their hands immediately upon entering a patient's room or being assigned trauma victims recently transferred onto the general unit who were challenging enough to those familiar with the hospital, but even more so to someone in a testing situation.

The ride to the hospital felt like self-inflicted torture to me. I had thoughts of getting off the van and disappearing. I had asked everyone I could think of to pray for me during this weekend, and I tried to dispel any negative images from my mind as best I could. Before leaving home, I had made a videotaped pep talk to myself and listened to it when I napped. Still, my hands were clammy. I had met my first evaluator the night before and hadn't felt at all comfortable with her. She didn't speak to me at all, except to explain my assignment and the diagnosis of my first patient. I had become very tense the night before in my hotel room and before falling asleep had read some passages concerning faith from Hugh Lynn Cayce's book *The Jesus I Knew* that helped me relax and fall asleep.

Before I knew it, there she was, my imposing evaluator, ready to lead me away into the unknown. As we walked to the nursing unit, she mentioned that there had been some "changes" in my required areas of care. My heart sank for a moment, fearing what that would mean, but soon I had reason for relief. It seems my patient for the morning had awakened early that day at 5:00 a.m. and requested that his bath and bed change be given. Those two simple nursing acts were now taken care of, and I could concentrate fully on the more difficult aspects of his care without as great a time element to worry about and without working up as much of a sweat.

He had fallen from a roof and suffered a collapsed lung; thus, he had chest tubes in place and was under the usual precautionary care given a head-injured person. He also had several intravenous lines going simultaneously, so his bath wouldn't have been a quick snap. I went about my duty carefully and with caution. Soon I had finished everything on my assignment sheet and had passed the first patient-care situation and could return to the cafeteria for a break before my next patient.

The rest of the weekend flowed smoothly, and it seemed that an unseen hand moved obstacles out of my way. The assignment of caring for a tiny baby changed from Saturday morning to Saturday afternoon, and he ate and slept peacefully as I performed my assessments. I later learned that he was very fussy in the mornings and obtaining a pulse on him was almost impossible because of his constant crying, a requirement that has failed students before. I had been spared! My final Sunday morning assignment was a man with multiple chronic health problems; he was in a very weakened state, and my evaluator advised me to encourage him to eat and move about more since he usually refused all care.

I took a deep breath and proceeded to dig within to eleven years of nursing experience to find the most appropriate way of reaching this very sick, Spanish-American man. Stepping to the side of his bed, I found a deeply jaundiced person, yellowed due to his chronic liver failure. Painfully thin, with parchment paper skin. His eyes were warm and friendly, though, and I took his hand to warm it when he complained that he was chilled. The phlebotomist entered and proceeded to try in vain to locate a feasible blood vessel suitable for the blood draw she needed. He grimaced in pain, and I stroked his shoulders. She gave up and obtained a specimen through a finger stick that required squeezing in order to get enough blood for the sample.

When his ordeal was over, he could have understandably wanted to lie back and refuse to move again, but he didn't. Instead, he cooperated beautifully with his morning care; even walking several feet to the nearby chair for breakfast. In his presence I forgot my nervousness and concentrated on helping him to the best of my ability. I walked out of that room ecstatic: passing this final component meant that the weekend was done! I breathed a prayer of thanks for this wonderful man who proved again that we nurses must be careful not to label our patients and expect difficulty just because of one hard day.

I quickly went to a phone booth to call my mom in Illinois. I knew she was on the edge of her seat, and as I made my way through the halls, I wanted to stop people and let them in on my wonderful news. Then, I attuned my ears to the music playing softly overhead—none other than Vivaldi's *Four Seasons,* the music that holds such special meaning to me about the power of God. I was truly floating on air!

I thought of the prayers that had gone out for me and of

the wondrous way the weekend reorganized itself to meet my needs. Then there were the dreams I had had so long ago counseling, "The Lord is my shepherd; I shall not want!" (Psalm 23:1) with mounting fury. I was living the truth of those words and knew it. I gave thanks. Later, Todd and I celebrated long into the night.

Over and over Jesus instructs His followers not to live in fear. The New Testament is full of His words concerning it. He placed such great emphasis on this that we have to ask ourselves why. What is it about fear—and worry is just a manifestation of that state—that is so detrimental to us? Looking to the readings for some illumination, I found: "One that is at times easily worried about material things. One that at times worries as respecting the application others make of their abilities. In the matter of worry, this—in its last analyses—is that of fear. Fear is an enemy to the mental development of an entity, changing or wavering the abilities of an entity in many directions." (2502-1)

This sounds as if the person receiving advice had difficulty not only with worrying about him/herself, but about what other people were doing—maybe an overprotective parent he or she was counseling? Perhaps not, but at any rate, it was someone who needed to release the propensity for worry lest his or her own "mental development" be stymied. There can be a great natural ability present in the individual, but worry has the potential for changing that.

This all might sound rather easier said than done and unrealistic to those who are facing catastrophic changes in their lives. How can you not help but think and worry about a child about to undergo open heart surgery? Or the loss of a job that's been the only work you knew for thirty years? Or a home that's been swept away by hurricane or flood?

This is where I make a distinction between concern and worry. I'm not suggesting we try to deny the circumstances facing us or repress them in some way. The concern we have for the people in our lives is undeniable and necessary. Concern looks for solutions and considers all the options. Concern offers prayers of thanks and asks for direction, spills its guts and cries. Worry ruminates over its constant stream of dreaded visions and becomes anxious beyond help at times. Concern deals with the task at hand and makes preparation for changes. Worry is either immobilized into inaction or acts too quickly out of fear.

As I said, I know about worry firsthand, because it is the way I dealt with the situations I had to meet for many years. The smallest thing could become a mountain in my mind after mulling it over for days. What I've found is that when the time came to actually face whatever the difficulty was, the strength was there in that moment. The anticipation was far worse than the actual problem. I stood in my own way and blocked my own creative potential by worrying.

I've never had to deal with a sick child or the loss of my home or job, but I have come up against some heart-stopping predicaments that tested me almost to my limit. One that I've already described was my early breakup with Tom. Another, my fear of functioning as a nurse with the AIDS epidemic rampant. Both times I had to take a day-by-day approach in living with the unknown, and second by second I was praying for release from the immobilizing hold my mind had on me.

I've watched courageous people in the middle of horrendous upheaval in their lives; what marks their courage is that they stand to face the enemy, daring to buck the odds and make it out on the other side stronger and more tender toward others. Since my husband specializes in physical medicine and rehabilitation, I am fortunate to meet many of life's heroes and heroines who come his way. One such example is a five-year-old girl named Amanda.

When she was only four years old, Amanda was critically injured in an automobile accident. Her mother's van went out of control and crashed into a tree, crushing Amanda's skull. The doctors gave her slim chances of survival and predicted blindness and severe mental deficits if she did. An entire side of her head was ripped open, and much of her brain damaged. Remarkably, she made it to rehab only three months later, and three months after that she went home!

I met her when she was almost ready to be discharged. During her time on the rehab unit she had made incredible advances; she is not blind, and she speaks in a tiny little girl's voice that could melt the most hardened heart. Her struggles to walk and use her "sleepy hand" in therapy were a great inspiration to the other patients there to work on their own recovery. They dubbed her "Amazing Amanda," an apt description, to say the least. She celebrated her fifth birthday on the nurse's station with a huge party organized by her mother, and I watched as she emanated love to all who came to wish her happiness. Shortly afterward she returned home.

The woman beside this darling girl was a strong, resilient person who kept the little one going with hugs and encouragement and untiring support. Her mother. Amanda's mom had lost her own mother not so long ago and was very well acquainted with heartache. While one cannot get inside another person's mind and heart to feel what she is feeling, I know that I marveled at how she kept her smile despite the strain this was causing her, with a younger son and husband many miles away. She stayed at the hospital championing each sign of progress that her child made, becoming an integral part of her healing. She had obviously not collapsed with worry; rather, she let her love and concern become a force for helping her daughter function once more.

Again, the wisdom from the readings: "One thing—remember this: Do not burden self with that as is unnecessary to be met until the time arises, for *worry* killeth. Labor strengthens—for through the efforts of the self *little* may be done, yet through that the body and the consciousness is able to direct *much* will be accomplished. As the necessary conditions arise, that as is best will be given thee." (900-345)

Jesus instructed us not to resist evil, and Herbert Bruce Puryear explains in his book *Why Jesus Taught Reincarnation* that when we are resisting something, we are actually building it into our subconscious by expending energy on it. (p. 37) Therefore, it follows that if instead of praying over a matter and attempting to work with what is at hand, we think it to death in our minds, we are making the problem worse. That means that not only does worry prevent us from seeing solutions, but it can actually be a big part of the problem.

It's a process of relearning how we deal with everything that comes our way. I'm working on it even now as I write, because uncertainties have come to roost once again (we always teach what we need to learn). Advice from the readings to a worry-prone individual was the use of this affirmation: "Here, Lord, am I. Use Thou me, this day, this evening, as Thou seest I may serve others the better; that I may so live, O God, to the glory of Thy name, Thy Son Jesus the Christ, and to the honor of mine own self in Thy name." (357-13)

Those words are truly a balm to my worry-worn mind. I have the tools, I am aware of the truth, but still I am a student struggling to practice what I preach. It has gotten less powerful, this fatal flaw of mine, as I use what I know. It used to be that fear and worry left me feeling like someone hanging and holding onto a rope, powerless. I thought that the world held the other end, but now I know that the Holy Spirit is there for me if I call and that I am not dangling helplessly as I imagined.

## 18

# Till We Meet Again

> "May the road rise up to meet you, may the wind always be at your back. May the sun shine warm upon your face, the rains fall soft upon your fields and, until we meet again, may God hold you in the palm of His hand." —Irish Blessing

KISSES and waves and cars pulling away; good-by is a well-worn word in my vocabulary. It has been uttered to people I've loved—to places I've lived. To my desire to have it my way. If my true intention is to have my will as one with Christ's, then my plans are subject to cancellation when I'm needed elsewhere by the Holy Spirit. There's a lesson in all of this, but at the moment it's occurring, it is difficult to bear sometimes. It seems to be one of my key assignments to learn to handle, since I'm faced with it so often. Good-by. The word carries a sadness within it, but one that I know is only temporary.

Throughout all of the farewells, see you soons, and so longs is a whispered phrase running as an undercurrent, gently pulling me along... "Follow Me." It is irresistible, and so I do follow, trusting that daily the appropriate marching orders will come. Throughout the journey, lives touch in the most amazing ways and then seem to veer apart. That's planet Earth for you, three dimensional and mired in materiality. Sometimes we move beyond it, though, and suddenly anything is possible, including the recognition that we can never really part.

Last night I dreamed... It was more than my typical assortment of symbols brought to life to teach or correct me. This one brought a visit from an old friend. We laughed and talked and touched in a way that made me feel that our spirits had truly communicated while we slept. I cherished this dream, because it was one of the few that reunited me with a childhood classmate taken from her friends far too early. She hasn't died, her body and spirit still move through each day in our hometown, but a serious accident left her with a severe brain injury that has silenced her for the last fifteen years.

When we first met, she brought joy and a sense of adventure to my seventh-grade life, and as I remember those times, I always see her smile. No one could help but love her, with her infectious optimism and shining golden hair, always ready for the next outrageous escapade. On our eighth-grade trip to Washington, D.C., our group of five girls sneaked cigarettes into the hotel room, stayed up all night smoking and giggling, and in general driving the chaperones crazy.

One night in our junior year of high school we spoke on the phone. We made arrangements to get together the next day, Saturday, to go downtown in my Volkswagen Bug, which I'd bought with money earned serving steaks at Ponderosa. She had a date for that Friday evening, and I was going to my brother and sister-in-law's house to watch television with my family. We joked, and I hung up the phone, oblivious to the knowledge that our relationship would soon change dramatically in the blink of an eye.

On the way home that night we heard sirens; they filled the air as we drove down Oakland Avenue. I wouldn't learn their destination until the next morning when the phone rang, breaking my dreamful sleep and rocking me out of my predictable schoolgirl life. While we had been making our way across town the night before, the car that Leslie was traveling in was turning into the path of a school bus on its way home from a ball game. The front-seat passenger was killed; Leslie, in the back seat, had received massive head injuries. Shock hung in the air as the unthinkable became real. That was in 1978.

It's tough for anyone to come face to face with the fragility of our human bodies. As a sixteen year old, I remember being frightened of the changes that Leslie had to endure as part of this sad drama. When it became clear that her recovery would not be complete, I experienced painfully the sum and substance of letting go. I still feel it when I wonder what it would be like to have her available to me now, to talk about men and movies and to laugh deep and hard with. Occasionally I am granted that delight when I drop the awareness of daily duties and waking reality to enter a sleep that brings a visit from her in perfect health and wholeness.

The losing of a friendship, or at least the particular form of it I am used to, is a bitter elixir to swallow, just as is moving away from someone I love. I sometimes question the why of things, but most of the time I trust the Master who sees the big picture with clearer vision than I have. We're each being prepared for a specific work and the necessary training is different for all of us. From the readings is this question: "For, each soul enters with a mission. And even as Jesus, the great missionary, we all have a mission to perform. Are we working with Him [continually], or just now and then? . . . For He faileth not. For He is ever the same, yesterday, today, tomorrow." (3003-1)

Part of the knowledge that I need to live out my mission is that each of us is connected inextricably, and separation is only a temporary clouding of the mind to our oneness. Also, the teaching and the admonition that only what we give away do we truly possess. This is a paradox, I realize, and a comforting one. The more I let go, the more I am free to really hold on! The moments that seem so fleeting are engraved in time forever. The love we share cannot ever die, and it is more than just a memory—it is more real than the earth we walk upon, more tangible than we can even intimate. My friend Leslie walked into my life a bright and glittering star, full of stories and excitement for living. She remains that way even though temporarily her light has changed focus, and she and I share a brief moment in time that is unalterable and cannot fall away.

The purpose that I have discovered which is central to my life is simply to walk a closer walk with Jesus and learn from Him how to really love. No matter where it takes me, no matter how many tears will fall. When I am alone—free of the many distractions I can become caught up in—I am more in tune with this part of my mission. He reveals a bit of the grand scheme in dosages small enough for me to handle. He leads me away, He leads me back. All the time holding my hand. Always taking gentle care of my heart.

When the time came for Tom and me to pack up and head for Bethlehem, once again a blessing was mixed with sorrow. The night before we were to leave, my mom had a little going-away party for me with family and friends present. My close friend Penny was there, along with a few others. After the barbecue and just before some of us were to go to a local nightclub to celebrate, I called Penny into my brother's garage so that I could pour out my feelings to her alone.

There was a dagger in my heart, and I felt as if I couldn't breathe. I was leaving my little nephews, and it was almost more than I could bear. I hadn't anticipated such an extreme reaction, and I wasn't prepared for it. Tears started to tumble out without my permission, and she tried her best to comfort me. I didn't want anyone else to see me breaking down, and she was one of the few with whom I felt comfortable letting it out. Her nature is the caring kind that wraps a blanket of warmth around an aching heart, and it helped just to grieve with her there. Then, putting it aside, I wiped my cheeks and went to the waiting car to be taken out dancing—something I was definitely not in the mood for.

Just then three-year-old Jeff came outside and yelled in his little boy's voice, "Are you going to Pen-sa-van-ya?" He didn't really know how far it was or when I would be with him again, but his question tore at me a little more. No, I reassured him for the moment; I'd be back later, and I'd see him in the morning.

The next morning he and Jason were still asleep when I went to say good-by, and I didn't wake them. I don't think I could have stood to say that word, I truly don't. Instead I entered the back porch of my brother's house with the dagger still firmly planted in my chest, twisting with my every move, and asked my sister-in-law to say my good-bys for me. Belief that the Holy Spirit engineered my move to Bethlehem helped ease the agony. Physical separation is probably the most difficult thing I've ever dealt with.

When the time comes to leave, as it always does, I must take deep breaths and literally step out with faith in the belief that I have given my life to God to be used as He pleases. I will walk wherever He leads, trusting that His ways are loving ways and He will not cause me any more pain than is necessary. It also helps to remember that one day there will be no more illusions of being apart. No more good-bys, no more tears.

I've been there to watch many brave ones in the ultimate act of letting go. It never gets easier, though, and when death visited my family, I felt the enigma of living and dying even more forcefully. My mom has two sisters, and ours is a close family. Her world was shaken the day she learned that her oldest sister Frances had cancer.

For months after learning of the grim diagnosis, pancreatic cancer, she tried to find ways of transmitting hope to Frances, to help her fight the good fight. She longed for the days gone by when she could have spent more time with her, but was caught up in her own life. Nothing I said to reassure her seemed to take root. Many mornings I would find her drinking her coffee and reading the paper through misty red eyes. Mom was helping me move from St. Louis after Tom had transferred to Florida. The phone rang just as we were putting the finishing touches on the apartment I was leaving, and the news from the other end was grim. The cancer had spread to the liver, and Frances's time would more than likely soon be gone. I uttered a prayer of thanks that circumstances had caused me to return to Decatur just when I would be needed most.

What hurts my mom, hurts me. I saw firsthand how crushing it is to live each day with impending death. I prayed and talked and hoped that she would be able to handle it when it came. I also worried for my grandma, a loving woman who always placed her family first and cared for them with a boundless energy. How could she face losing her first-born child?

Soon Frances became bedridden, and the narcotics that helped ease her pain made it difficult for her to stay awake long enough to talk. My mom visited as frequently as she could. Together we sat by her bed for a while on Christmas Eve, talking the usual family talk of presents and plans for the holiday. She seemed comfortable and at peace through the haze of the painkillers; pale and frail, yet still a beautiful woman lying there in her silky gown. It was the last time I would see my aunt. On a cold day in the middle of January, surrounded by her family—mother, sisters, husband, and daughters—my Aunt Frances passed through the door we know as death. Many tears were shed, as we groped for the way to say good-by.

When Jesus learned of Lazarus's death, the Bible tells us that He wept (John 11:35). These tears fell despite the fact that He had known that death was imminent and that He intended to raise him from the dead, which He subsequently did! When I read of this incident, it only serves to impress me even more deeply with the knowledge that being here on the earth in flesh and blood hurts. It cuts beyond skin and muscle and even beyond the heart we so often feel shattering. It cuts to the essence of our being. We can't wish it away, but we can share it with the Master, who knows the pain intimately, as well as how to ease it.

Frances's entire family reached out to one another in the sadness of her death. My cousin later shared with me that she had dreamed many times about losing her watch before learning of her mom's cancer diagnosis. Indeed, her time in this life had ended. Knowing that her spirit lives on is comforting, but cannot displace the necessary mourning that comes when that transformation is made.

All that I could do was try to reassure my mom through listening and reinforcing her belief in the eternal nature of the soul. Believing that one day we will see once more the ones we've lost is a soothing oil of hope that eases but does not eliminate the hurting. Living without that conviction is inconceivable to me.

The time of release comes to us all many times: through death, disability, divorce, and leaving home. One of the few things I am absolutely convinced of is that when I gave my will to Jesus and asked that He guide me through it all, He has done exactly that. When Tom's grandfather died during that demanding period of his medical training, I was there with him to help. At the time of my brother's divorce, I was able to be back home where I was needed, just as I was during Aunt Frances's illness and death.

There have been happy surprises as well, like finding Tom and other unforgettable friends such as Virginia, the Milwaukee brothers, Henry, and Micki. Always, though, I have been able to rely on Him for the travel plan. But when it's time for good-by, it's not without tears.

Closing my eyes, I see this vision:

> In the late afternoon sun a gathering of thousands waits for the doors to open to the elaborate banquet hall. Smiling, hearts racing with anticipation, they wear the look of complete happiness and contentment. Seven o'clock chimes, and the huge doors burst wide open. In barely restrained order they file in to find each one's table, filled to overflowing with food and drink.
>
> They all are pleased to hear their favorite music and taste their best-loved dinnertime treats. As they find their seats, they are astonished and overcome with joy to meet once again husbands, fathers, sisters, mothers, daughters, sons, brothers, uncles, cousins, aunts, and every friend they've ever known.
>
> I find my table and see my aunt and my grandfather waiting with dancing eyes and words of welcome for all of us. Turning around, there is Leslie, talking nonstop to her sisters about some gorgeous guy at the end of the hall. I peek over to find my old friend Henry, dancing with his bride, spinning and lifting her off the ground in jubilation! Harriet bends to let me hear her voice for the first time face to face. Path-crossers I never thought I'd see again are sprinkled throughout, and I make my way to each one in loving embrace.

Someday, it has to be. Someday we will share in Mary Magdalene's elation that long-ago morning as the sun began to caress the land and Jeshua, missing from the tomb, whispered her name. When the reality dawns that we are all alive and fully conscious of our divine relationship to one another, a celebration wilder than the ability to imagine will break out. What heaven! What grand things we have to look forward to!

For all those I've loved dearly or known briefly, who have brought me closer to the realization that we are all one people, connected by Love—you have touched me in ways deeper than even I know. I thank you for that gift and look so forward to when next we meet.

# ABOUT THE AUTHOR

Carolyn Kresse Murray became a nurse in 1982 at age twenty. Her growth as health-care provider has been highly influenced by the spiritual practices that she undertook while in nursing school. She has worked in a variety of settings, including hospitals, nursing homes, and home care. She earned her B.A. in management in 1991. She is also involved in rehabilitation nursing and is a member of the Association of Rehabilitation Nurses.

Carolyn has been a student of the Edgar Cayce psychic readings since childhood. Active in the Search for God study group program for many years, she has put into practice the disciplines that the Cayce readings encourage—particularly those of meditation and prayer. A registered nurse, she has also applied both the spiritual and physical recommendations found in the Cayce work as she goes about her chosen career. Throughout this time she has discovered that the spiritual path is not only deeply meaningful, but adventurous as well.

Carolyn currently lives with her husband, Tom, an M.D., in Ponte Vedra, Florida, where she is a nurse, author, and teacher.

## What Is A.R.E.?

The Association for Research and Enlightenment, Inc. (A.R.E.®), is the international headquarters for the work of Edgar Cayce (1877-1945), who is considered the best-documented psychic of the twentieth century. Founded in 1931, the A.R.E. consists of a community of people from all walks of life and spiritual traditions, who have found meaningful and life-transformative insights from the readings of Edgar Cayce.

Although A.R.E. headquarters is located in Virginia Beach, Virginia—where visitors are always welcome—the A.R.E. community is a global network of individuals who offer conferences, educational activities, and fellowship around the world. People of every age are invited to participate in programs that focus on such topics as holistic health, dreams, reincarnation, ESP, the power of the mind, meditation, and personal spirituality.

In addition to study groups and various activities, the A.R.E. offers membership benefits and services, a bimonthly magazine, a newsletter, extracts from the Cayce readings, conferences, international tours, a massage school curriculum, an impressive volunteer network, a retreat-type camp for children and adults, and A.R.E. contacts around the world. A.R.E. also maintains an affiliation with Atlantic University, which offers a master's degree program in Transpersonal Studies.

For additional information about A.R.E. activities hosted near you, please contact:

A.R.E.
67th St. and Atlantic Ave.
P.O. Box 595
Virginia Beach, VA 23451-0595
(804) 428-3588

### A.R.E. Press

A.R.E. Press is a publisher and distributor of books, audiotapes, and videos that offer guidance for a more fulfilling life. Our products are based on, or are compatible with, the concepts in the psychic readings of Edgar Cayce.

We especially seek to create products which carry forward the inspirational story of individuals who have made practical application of the Cayce legacy.

For a free catalog, please write to A.R.E. Press at the address below or call toll free 1-800-723-1112. For any other information, please call 804-428-3588.

> A.R.E. Press
> Sixty-Eighth & Atlantic Avenue
> P.O. Box 656
> Virginia Beach, VA 23451-0656

# Discover for Yourself

## the Wealth of Insights Contained in the Edgar Cayce Material...

Throughout his life, Edgar Cayce (1877-1945) was able to display powers of perception that extended beyond the five senses. He was guided by one solitary goal: to be helpful to people, and he used his talents of psychic perception to provide practical guidance for thousands of individuals.

The Edgar Cayce legacy contains information on more than 10,000 different subjects in the areas of healing, holistic health, spirituality, meditation, philosophy, reincarnation, dream interpretation, and prophecy. He has been called a philosopher, the most gifted psychic of all times, and the father of the holistic health movement. More than 300 books have been written about his work!

In 1931, Cayce founded the Association for Research and Enlightenment, Inc. (A.R.E.) to study and research this information. Today, the A.R.E. is an open-membership organization–made up of thousands of individuals around the world–that offers conferences, seminars, research projects, newsletters, and small group activities. For information, call 1-800-333-4499, or use the card below.

☐ Enroll me as a member of A.R.E. (Edgar Cayce's Association for Research and Enlightenment, Inc.) I enclose $40.00 (Outside U.S.A. add $15.00 postage.)

**VISA or Master Card CALL TOLL FREE
1-800-333-4499, 24 hours a day, 7 days a week**

*You may cancel at any time and receive a full refund on all unmailed benefits.*

OR Make check or money order payable to A.R.E. (Non-U.S. residents must make payment in United States funds.)

☐ Check or Money Order  ☐ MasterCard  ☐ VISA

*If payment is enclosed, please use envelope for your privacy.*

Expiration Date: Mo. ___ Yr. ___   1712

Charge Card Number: ☐☐☐☐ – ☐☐☐☐ – ☐☐☐☐ – ☐☐☐☐

Signature _____
(Important! Sign here to use credit card.)

Name (please print) _____
Address _____
City _____ State _____ Zip _____
Phone ( ___ ) _____

☐ I can't join right now, but please send me additional information about A.R.E. activities, publications, and membership.

## *How Can I Participate in A.R.E.?*

Although A.R.E. Headquarters is located in Virginia Beach, Virginia–where visitors are always welcome– the A.R.E. is a global network of individuals in more than seventy countries. The underlying principle of the Edgar Cayce readings is the oneness of all life, tolerance for all people, and a compassion and understanding for individuals of all faiths, races, and backgrounds.

In addition to Headquarters, hundreds of study groups and Edgar Cayce Centers exist world-wide. Regardless of your location, individuals are invited to participate in group activities, explore new publications, or simply enjoy membership benefits through the mail.

For additional information about the organization's activities and services, please use the card below or contact:

A.R.E., 67th Street & Atlantic Ave.
P.O. Box 595, Virginia Beach, VA 23451-0595

### *The Wealth of Insights Contained in the Edgar Cayce Material Includes:*

| | | |
|---|---|---|
| *Alternative Healing Principles* | *Universal Laws* | *Global Community* |
| *Dreams* | *Attitudes & Emotions* | *ESP* |
| *Spiritual Healing* | *Mysticism* | *Self-Hypnosis* |
| *Study Groups* | *Karma & Grace* | *Death & Dying* |
| *Earth Changes* | *Meditation* | *Prophecy* |
| *Psychic Development* | *Spiritual Guidance* | *Astrology* |
| *Atlantis & Ancient Civilizations* | *Reincarnation* | *Akashic Records* |
| *Discovering Your Soul's Purpose* | *Angels* | *And Hundreds More...* |

---

EDGAR CAYCE FOUNDATION and
A.R.E. LIBRARY/VISITORS CENTER
Virginia Beach, Virginia
*Serving You Since 1931*

NO POSTAGE
NECESSARY
IF MAILED
IN THE
UNITED STATES

**BUSINESS REPLY MAIL**
FIRST CLASS MAIL PERMIT NO. 2456, VIRGINIA

POSTAGE WILL BE PAID BY ADDRESSEE

A.R.E.®
P.O. Box 595
Virginia Beach, VA 23451-9909